RESURRECTION

SHOCK

Background Guide

LANE SANFORD WEBSTER

IF CHRIST HAS NOT BEEN RAISED, OUR PREACHING IS USELESS AND SO IS YOUR FAITH. MORE THAN THAT, WE ARE THEN FOUND TO BE FALSE WITNESSES ABOUT GOD, FOR WE HAVE TESTIFIED ABOUT GOD THAT HE RAISED CHRIST FROM THE DEAD ... IF THE DEAD ARE NOT RAISED, "LET US EAT AND DRINK, FOR TOMORROW WE DIE."

— Paul of Tarsus, ex-persecutor turned tireless apostle, from his letter circa AD 55, 1 Corinthians 15:13–15, 32 quoting Isaiah 22:13 (NIV)

RESURRECTION

SHOCK

Background Guide

LANE SANFORD WEBSTER

WestBow
PRESS®
A DIVISION OF THOMAS NELSON
& ZONDERVAN

This book is a work of non-fiction. Unless otherwise noted, the author and the publisher make no explicit guarantees as to the accuracy of the information contained in this book and in some cases, names of people and places have been altered to protect their privacy.

WestBow Press books may be ordered through booksellers or by contacting:

WestBow Press
A Division of Thomas Nelson & Zondervan
1663 Liberty Drive
Bloomington, IN 47403
www.westbowpress.com
844-714-3454

Scriptures taken from the Holy Bible, New International Version®, NIV®. Copyright © 1973, 1978, 1984, 2011 by Biblica, Inc.™ Used by permission of Zondervan. All rights reserved worldwide. www.zondervan.com The "NIV" and "New International Version" are trademarks registered in the United States Patent and Trademark Office by Biblica, Inc.™

ISBN: 978-1-9736-6712-4 (sc)
ISBN: 978-1-9736-6713-1 (e)

Print information available on the last page.

WestBow Press rev. date: 09/04/2020

To Brooke

who knows why

ACKNOWLEDGMENTS

rateful am I for the friends, family members, colleagues, and teachers who reviewed this background guide, gave me their honest responses, and made more than a few worthy suggestions. Nevertheless, any errors, omissions, lapses in judgment, or other residual faults remain solely my own.

When barely embryonic, the overall project concept was incubated about three years ago when I presented it informally to notables of the Regent College community in Vancouver, B.C. Canada: Dr. Sven Soderlund, a New Testament professor who taught an epic seminar on the book of Hebrews; Dr. Donald Lewis, professor of Christian history, who originally befriended me in Oxford, England when I was an untutored lad on a year abroad; and a scholar in his own right, Bill Reimer, who for many years has guided with distinction what I still consider my happiest indoor place on earth, the Regent College Bookstore.

Those who read a version of this background guide, in addition to the main book, displayed uncustomary valor: Berkely Webster, Dr. J. Carl Laney, Dr. Lambert Dolphin and Dr. Marvin D. Webster, my father, veteran pastor and valued leader on seminary and missions boards. At key intervals in the journey, further encouragement came from Dean Christensen, Merit Webster, Robert Bouzon, Tegan Webster, and my mother, Virginia L. Webster, compassionate teacher and classical, worshipful keyboardist. One other credit is due. Now gone to glory, Dr. Ray C. Stedman unknowingly influenced these pages when he took me aside for a season as a young man in Palo Alto, California and grounded me in a biblical strata of bedrock spiritual truths that continue to reverberate in my heart and mind. My gratitude goes out to all these exemplary people who have helped bring this extended endeavor to the light of day.

RESURRECTION

SHOCK

Background Guide

LANE SANFORD WEBSTER

CONTENTS

ABBREVIATIONS

OLD TESTAMENT

Gen.	Genesis
Ex.	Exodus
Lev.	Leviticus
Num.	Numbers
Deut.	Deuteronomy
Josh.	Joshua
Judg.	Judges
Ruth	Ruth
1–2 Sam.	1–2 Samuel
1–2 Kings	1–2 Kings
1–2 Chron.	1–2 Chronicles
Ezra	Ezra
Neh.	Nehemiah
Esther	Esther
Job	Job
Ps.	Psalms
Prov.	Proverbs
Eccles.	Ecclesiastes
Song	Song of Songs
Isa.	Isaiah
Jer.	Jeremiah
Lam.	Lamentations
Ezek.	Ezekiel
Dan.	Daniel
Hos.	Hosea
Joel	Joel
Amos	Amos
Obad.	Obadiah
Jon.	Jonah
Mic.	Micah
Nah.	Nahum
Hab.	Habakkuk
Zeph.	Zephaniah
Hag.	Haggai
Zech.	Zechariah
Mal.	Malachi

ABBREVIATIONS

NEW TESTAMENT

Mt	Matthew
Mk	Mark
Lk	Luke
Jn	John
Acts	Acts
Rom.	Romans
1–2 Cor.	1–2 Corinthians
Gal.	Galatians
Eph.	Ephesians
Phil.	Philippians
Col.	Colossians
1–2 Thess.	1–2 Thessalonians
1–2 Tim.	1–2 Timothy
Titus	Titus
Philemon	Philemon
Heb.	Hebrews
James	James
1–2 Pet.	1–2 Peter
1–3 Jn	1–3 John
Jude	Jude
Rev.	Revelation

INTRODUCTION

PURPOSE OF THE
BACKGROUND GUIDE

Welcome to this further investigation of the resurrection of Jesus. You are reading the background guide to the book called, *"Resurrection Shock: Did the Disciples Get It Right?"* This guide is a supplement to the main book, not a sequel or second volume, nor a book that stands on its own. The purpose of the main book is to show how the accounts from eyewitnesses, and from the first-century writers who record their reports, amount to a set of compelling lines of historical evidence for the resurrection of Jesus. Wherever possible, you are invited to look over the shoulders of the various eyewitnesses, then to consider for yourself to what extent these people appear to be credible. We can assess an extra measure of credibility for those witnesses where the historical evidence permits us to track how they proceeded in their lives to live out their belief in the resurrection of Jesus that they proclaimed to others.

The approach of the main book is designed for general readers, not so much for the academic world (even though the evidence presented applies to inquiries from either sector). However, certain issues in our resurrection investigation are determined by fairly tedious historical methods. These methods tend to bog down a reader who wants to evaluate the content of the evidence more than the process of historiography. Yet it strikes me that some readers may want more historical evaluation of the sources used in the main book. Or they may want more historical background on some related, though arguably tangential issues that may pop up in the reader's mind. Sometimes such questions slow or even detour the journey, like an irritating burr in a horse's saddle. Some readers, if these more nuanced issues are not even addressed, let alone fully resolved, find themselves unable to concentrate on the book's major lines of evidence for the resurrection. Also, in the event that a group is working through the book, at least a few are likely to be bothered by such questions. Therefore, this information may help group leaders keep the whole crew going forward by getting answers or at least some definition and context on these issues. Out of these considerations, I have offered this supplement to the main book, and given it the simple title, *Resurrection Shock: Background Guide*.

Briefly, let me walk you through the sections in the guide, which are denoted as "resources." Each resource is a separate entry, and really might be placed in any order, so I use the term "resource" rather than chapter. Let me describe these to you succinctly.

The first resource gives background on the major source documents for the resurrection lines of evidence in the main book, chapters 1–9. Most (though not all) of the sources are found in the collection of 27 documents known as the New Testament. I take up issues of authorship and major content in these selected writings. Then, I briefly explain how a series of later writings do not pass historical muster and cannot serve as serious parts of our investigation. All this is in resource 1, "Sorting Out the Sources."

How the original manuscripts—for the documents on which we are relying—can be dated is the issue in resource 2, "Estimating Document Dates." Related to these first two resources is a third background essay on our sources. Earlier this backgrounder was placed in this guide, but then I decided to put it in the main book, due to the importance of the subject. It shows how the documents behind the resurrection narrative measure up to typical secular criteria for historical reliability. It contends that these sources, despite the theological motivation on the part of their writers, nevertheless carry strong historical evidence that can be evaluated alongside other documents from that era. You can find it in the main book in the additions section as addition 3, "Measuring the Resurrection Narrative by Historical Criteria."

Aside from the issues of sources and authors, and validity of the overall narrative, some specific historical questions naturally arise in our resurrection investigation. One of these is the year when the death and alleged resurrection of Jesus occurs. For some readers, that year can be either a curiosity or an unsettling concern, due to some supposed discrepancies in the gospels. As a result, we dive in and discuss some options on how to determine that timeline in resource 3, "Calculating Timelines for Resurrection Week and Year."

One of the key lines of evidence for the resurrection asserts that Jesus fulfills Old Testament prophecy (chapter 9). For that line, a major prophecy comes in the book of Isaiah, dealing with the servant figure. This figure has been subject to alternative interpretations throughout history, especially from the Jewish rabbinic communities. As a result, I address this in resource 4, "Reviewing Rabbinic Takes on the Servant in Isaiah." This resource contrasts and compares several major interpretations to the one I present in the main book. Another issue arises over the first-century Jewish cultural assumptions about group resurrection in the end times. When the disciples preached the resurrection of Jesus, they proclaim it in a cultural context that had clear expectations of a group resurrection already. What those expectations were in the Jewish mind-set of Jesus's time on earth is covered in resource 5, "Surveying Jewish Expectations of Resurrection."

This supplemental book ends with the resource (denoted as resource 6), "Found in the Ground Archaeological Index." In the main book, archaeological findings that support the resurrection lines of evidence are sprinkled through the text of the main chapters, in windows or boxes (also known sometimes as sidebars). Some boxes cover other categories, including historical portals, bible sidelights, interpretive angles and textual details. When it is an archaeological finding in view in the box, it shows "Found in the Ground" in the first category line. Then the last line has an index number. That number matches the numbers for entries in this index. These index entries extend the brief descriptions in the boxes in the main chapters. The entries also cite specific references (many of them easily accessible online) should the reader want to delve more deeply into some of these startling discoveries that have been literally found in the ground, mainly over the last two centuries. Most of the major, current archaeological findings for the NT documents appear in this index. That makes it a valuable resource in itself, for other studies involving biblical documents.

Because issues continually arise in research on the resurrection, this supplemental book may add other resources in future editions. For now, the resources included here address specific questions and are intended to provide some clear avenues for answers. My hope is that you will find these resources illuminating and maybe even inspiring as you explore the historical evidence for the resurrection of Jesus.

Lane Sanford Webster
Autumn 2019

NOTE

ON STRUCTURE AND USAGE

As noted earlier, this book is designed as a supplement to the main book, *Resurrection Shock: Did the Disciples Get It Right?* The main book presents nine lines of evidence for the resurrection of Jesus, in nine chapters (with a tenth chapter that assesses alternative theories that deny that the resurrection happened). This guide follows the same stylistic aspects as the main book.

In the interest of clarity, allow me to explain briefly some of the particular terminology employed in this guide.

Counting the Years

We are taking a historical approach, but I do not use the terms for dating years now common in historical research. Most historians now use BCE to stand for years Before the Common Era instead of BC, Before Christ. Accordingly, they like to use CE to stand for "in the Common Era" instead of AD, the Latin abbreviation for *anno Domini*, "in the year of our Lord," counting from the estimated year of the birth of Jesus. We will stay with the traditional BC and AD. It is just easier, and this book is meant for the general reader. Be assured that in either notation scheme, the numbers for the years remain the same.

Most historians now agree Jesus was born several years before the commonly held year (AD 1) of his birth, but that does not change the accepted point from which the years in history continue to be counted. When years cannot be precisely determined to a single year or two, I use "c." for "circa," meaning the action occurred around the estimated year though not necessarily in that year exactly. A "d." means the estimated year a figure from history died.

Measurement Systems

For measurements, I give distance measurements in terms of miles and kilometers and size measurements in feet or inches (ft or in) and in meters or centimeters (m or cm), usually not spelling out the measurement indicator in full. Including both systems offloads the calculation readers otherwise might have to make.

Source Abbreviations

To reduce repetition, I usually abbreviate references to gospel verses with two-letter indicators without periods (Mk for Mark, Mt for Matthew, Lk for Luke, Jn for John) with chapter and verse separated conventionally by a colon. Other biblical books are referred to either by their full names such as Acts or by common abbreviations with periods such as 1 Cor. for 1 Corinthians.

When I provide an exact quotation (from the Bible or from another original source) separate from the main text in block form, I spell out the full name of the book. Usually, the New Testament is abbreviated as NT and the Old Testament as OT. For some readers, the term *old* may carry a negative connotation. It should be understood as the testament coming earlier, the first testament. The Jewish term for it is the Tanakh; the term is used increasingly in academia but is not yet common among general readers. Two works outside the NT also are denoted in the main text with abbreviations. These two come from the Jewish-Roman author Josephus, also known as Flavius Josephus, a new first name he obtained once he started schmoozing with Roman royalty. I abbreviate his book the *Antiquities of the Jews* with the numbers following it for book, chapter, and paragraph, for example (*Antiquities* 18.9.2). His book *The Jewish War* (or *Wars*) is abbreviated similarly (*War* 17.6.3).

Citations

Books and journal articles have long had clearly established practices for citation, and here we mainly use the Chicago style format. Regarding websites, we frequently run into missing pieces for citations when the practices for online resources are not as yet fully standardized. You may see the following terms: n.a. for no author, n.d. for no date, and n.p. for no publisher when any of these are unattainable.

Wikipedia offers no authors' names and rarely dates, so article titles are the primary identifier in these citations. I cite Wikipedia mainly as a source for well-known facts but rarely for interpretations.

I do not bother to provide complicated URL tracking codes because keyword searches on the internet almost always locate the source with the current advances in search technology.

Italics

As is customary, italics are used in the text to emphasize a word or phrase. I also use italics in webpage citations for the *publisher,* and in books for the *title* of the book. Quotations from the Bible or from other sources are rendered in italics in block form, and also usually in italics when they appear in the main text, in order to highlight the material from original sources. In a few instances where I relate what is likely going on in the mind of a biblical person, their surmised thoughts also are shown in italics.

That should do it. Now you are all set to dive into whichever issues most strike your interest. There is no particular sequence to the resources in this supplement, so start wherever you wish as you continue to explore personally the historical evidence for the resurrection of Jesus.

REFERENCE

CONTENTS OF
Resurrection Shock: Did the Disciples Get It Right?

H ere for your reference is a reprint showing the contents in the main book, *Resurrection Shock: Did the Disciples Get It Right?* In this supplement, the resources often refer you to one of the chapters or additions as listed below. To avoid confusion, we do not list the page numbers here, but certainly you can find them in the table of contents in the main book.

CONTENTS

RESOURCE

1

SORTING OUT THE SOURCES

T he witness accounts of the resurrection are collected in first-century AD documents. Our lines of evidence in the chapters in the main book derive from these documents. Since we are taking a historical approach, like historians we need to assess our sources. Here I provide basic background information on the authors of these documents, an overview of their content, and a sense of their composition process.

The following writers and their writings are covered in this order: Paul, Luke (his process), Mark, Matthew, Luke (his gospel), John (his gospel), Luke (his historical account, Acts), Peter (his two letters), John (his first letter), James, the author of Hebrews, and Josephus (his two histories, neither of which is in the Bible). These writers with their selected documents provide us with reasonably reliable sources for the lines of evidence for the resurrection and resulting events. Added at the end is a review of documents circulating later than these first-century accounts. Most of these later documents that I list are written within the next two centuries, but few if any beyond that period. I offer brief descriptions and some of the problems they present, pointing to why they are not historically reliable as reports of either the resurrection or its witnesses.

Paul: His Letters Turn into NT Books

The earliest document asserting the resurrection of Jesus comes to us in a letter from a tentmaker by trade turned missionary by calling named Paul. Paul in many ways is the best-known personality—or second best, if we include Jesus—in the first-century world. Partly this is due to Luke spending the second half of his historical work, the book of Acts, narrating primarily the adventures of Paul on the Mediterranean mission field. Partly also this level of prominence is due to Paul's own writings. His writings all fit into the genre of personal letters to faith communities. His letters comprise traditionally thirteen of the 27 "books" or documents in the New Testament. Of these thirteen letters attributed to Paul, seven are considered to be from him beyond dispute, while six remain in scholarly debate to one degree or another. For the purposes of this investigation, I reference data about Paul primarily from the letters not in dispute (1 and 2 Corinthians, Romans, Galatians, Philippians, 1 Thessalonians, Philemon). For the others in dispute (Ephesians, Colossians, 2 Thessalonians, 1 and 2 Timothy, and Titus, all of which your author accepts as authoritative and canonical), I will not bother debating their origins here, due to our laser focus on the resurrection narrative.

Before becoming a Christian missionary to Greek-speaking cities, Paul in his late twenties occupies himself as a Jewish scholar, activist and doctrinal enforcer in Jerusalem. He has close access to the high priests. His personal journey in and of itself is one line of evidence for the resurrection of Jesus (see chapter 6).

His letter to Christian believers in the Greek city of Corinth, probably written from the major city of Ephesus across the Aegean Sea, is solidly dated to AD 55 (see chapter 7 for the data behind this established date). In it, Paul reinforces the core of their faith. At one key point, in broad brushstrokes, Paul gives the basic sequence of the resurrection account (1 Cor. 15:3–8). Jesus dies, he is buried, he is raised, and he appears to a wide range of eyewitnesses, some of whom Paul specifically names (see chapters 2 and 7). He includes himself among those who have personal interactions with the risen Jesus. Actually, his interaction is different from the other appearances that happen *before* Jesus ascends. Paul's event comes through an intervention *after* Jesus leaves earth. It still counts as resurrection evidence, especially in light of the turnaround it causes in Paul's life. This passage is one of the bedrock sections in the entire NT collection. Together with Luke's report of Peter's pioneering message (Acts 2:14–41), and Paul's recap of his own early conversion (Gal. 1:13–2:10), it forms the key equation to prove that the preaching of the resurrection of Jesus was not a later development in history but virtually immediate. Importantly, it debunks the theory that the resurrection of Jesus was a mere legend layered up over multiple generations (see chapter 7).

Nonetheless, in his letters, Paul spends almost no time detailing the activities and teachings of Jesus. The absence of this data is understandable. Paul did not experience these moments himself. His overarching concern is to work out how Jesus fulfills the destiny of the nation of Israel, and in so doing, how Jesus offers salvation and new life to all nations of the world. Paul wants people to know how Jesus's death and resurrection usher in a new era where people from all nations can come into a relationship with the one true God. He is focused on the *results* of the resurrection. He is keen to explain how believers can live by the power of the indwelling Spirit of God, and grow close to God. He also wants to show them how they can build community and live in harmony with one another and with outsiders.

Consequently, Paul for the most part works from what he considers to be *the fact* of Jesus's death and resurrection (2 Cor. 4:10–14; Rom. 6:5–11, 8:11). He takes it as his starting point, as condensed in the creed he receives and passes on to the people in Corinth (1 Cor. 15:3–23, see chapter 7).

The Gospels: The Documents Compile Witness Accounts

Despite being our earliest writer, Paul does not give us details of Jesus's ministry in Galilee, as noted above. He does not illustrate how compelling and memorable Jesus's teaching was, how he trains his often slow-on-the-uptake disciples, or how events lead up to his arrest, trial, excruciating death and alleged miraculous comeback. For this type of information, we have other documents. They belong to the genre commonly called "gospel," meaning "good news."

In fact, we have four NT gospels.[1] In the major aspects of the death, burial and resurrection of Jesus the four accounts concur. One of the only exceptions comes with the appearances by Jesus after his resurrection, which figure prominently in three gospel accounts, but are missing in Mark (see chapter 2).

Now not so fast, the trained historians object. It is not enough just to look at the content in the writings, comparing and contrasting. The historian wants to ask more questions about the writers themselves. Where did they get their information? Who were they as people, as best we can ascertain? When did they write? Are they operating independently of each other?[2]

These questions asked of ancient documents are much harder to answer because there was a tradition for authors not to identify themselves, not to date their works, and not to credit or catalog any sources they utilize.

---

[1] Quite a few other so-called "gospels" were circulated but did not pass muster to the extent that they could be included in the recognized Christian canon. Among these were the supposed gospels of Peter, Thomas, Mary and Judas. Each had its own peculiar form of undoing. See the later section in this resource on the documents not selected, for their clear and sometimes comical deficiencies.

[2] For more detail on dating documents, see resource 2 in this guide. For more data on how the documents combine to meet standard historical criteria, and therefore how they support a reliable resurrection narrative, see the main book *Resurrection Shock,* addition 3.

Luke: The Author Delineates the Process of Writing a Gospel

We are in luck however with the biography of Jesus which is commonly called the gospel of Luke. Luke does not identify himself as the author in either the gospel of Luke or in his sequel, Acts. Luke's name is attached later by succeeding generations of Christian leaders who vouch for him as the author.[3] He is mentioned by name in the NT in letters attributed to Paul, as one of Paul's close and most loyal associates (Philemon 24; Col. 4:14; 2 Tim. 4:11). On Paul's second extended journey, Luke meets up with him at Troas. The city is on the eastern Aegean Sea. It is a major port for crossing over to Greece, and possibly Luke's hometown. Luke then travels frequently with Paul, including the hazardous voyage to Rome from Caesarea (see chapter 6). Luke is identified as a medical doctor (Col. 4:14). His prose shows that he is highly educated and that Greek almost certainly is his first language. He likely is the only non-Jewish author in the NT, for conspicuously he is not mentioned among the circumcised in one incidental list (Col. 4:10–11, 14).

In the preamble to his first book, his gospel, Luke offers a few clues about his writing's purpose and process, as well as his patron.

> *Many have undertaken to draw up an account of the things that have been fulfilled among us, just as they were handed down to us by those who from the first were eyewitnesses and servants of the word. With this in mind, since I myself have carefully investigated everything from the beginning, I too decided to write an orderly account for you, most excellent Theophilus, so that you may know the certainty of the things you have been taught. (Luke 1:1-4)*

---

[3] Luke is identified as the author of a gospel and the book of Acts by the Muratorian Canon (c. AD 170) and by the early Christian writer Irenaeus, as well as others listed by Eusebius (c. AD 325) in his *Church History*, 3.4.

The name Theophilus has the meaning "lover of God." This meaning has led some to assert that it is a generic term for a believer. Yet it is a common Greek name. So most scholars conclude it addresses an individual, probably the affluent patron or publisher of Luke's book. Luke is clear that his purpose is to bring *"certainty"* to the things that have been *"taught"* or *"believed."* The written word by definition makes things more specific and more stable, so that any reader can consult the document as needed. Just by writing, Luke locks in the information and brings more stability. The greater certainty also derives from the way he researches. *"I myself have carefully investigated everything from the beginning."* Luke claims he has been meticulous and comprehensive. Also, he adds another goal, to produce an *"orderly account."* Luke mentions he is not the first to attempt this task. *"Many have undertaken to draw up an account,"* he notes. We can surmise that Luke has read other accounts and not been satisfied by them, so he says, *"I too decided to write."* The other accounts likely were not measuring up to his standards. To his mind, they were not ordered properly, not comprehensive or not carefully researched. However, the fact that he mentions other accounts, shows that he is working with some written materials in order to produce his own.

As part of his research, Luke also indicates that he has spoken directly with eyewitnesses. Reports about what happened with Jesus *"were handed down to us."* These are not just secondhand. These probably include firsthand reports told to him *"by those who from the first were eyewitnesses and servants of the word."* Eyewitnesses would include not only the inner circle of handpicked disciples, but also the larger entourage that accompanies Jesus, including many women (Lk 24:9-10, 33; Acts 1:14-15). Luke probably could access other witnesses, such as Manaen, a Christian later based in Antioch, who was raised alongside Herod Antipas (Acts 13:1). The term *"servants of the word"* would likely refer to teachers in the early church (Lk 6:2-4). Initially, these teachers are drawn from Jesus's select band of original disciples. Prominent among them would be Peter and John. In both NT letters attributed to him, Peter asserts his experience as an eyewitness (1 Pet. 5:1; 2 Pet.1:16–18), as does John in his first letter (1 Jn 1:1).

In this short yet telling preamble, Luke makes clear he is basing his account on highly reputable sources. He clarifies that he is not himself an eyewitness. But he has been in contact with multiple witnesses and reviewed other writings that have tried to capture the content of Jesus's life.

Can we identify any of those other written accounts that Luke may have used? We can, at least some of them. Scholars call this source analysis. One source for the gospel of Luke that they have identified is, lo and behold, the gospel of Mark. About half of the book of Mark is contained in the book of Luke (with Matthew using even more of Mark).[4]

Luke's drawing on Mark should come as no surprise, for a couple of reasons. Luke has said he consulted other accounts. He would know if Mark produced an account because he and Mark were colleagues. In two letters they are mentioned together, as Paul's associates (Philemon 24; 2 Tim 4:11). Also, Luke as a writer displays a sophisticated style with the Greek language. In passages where he uses material from Mark, he sometimes upgrades the grammar or explains matters Mark leaves hanging (as does Matthew).[5] This tendency, along with the preamble evidence mentioning other prior writings, indicates that Luke uses Mark as a source, rather than the other way around. Moreover, Luke sets forth a stated goal to produce an orderly account; in contrast, Mark is scolded by an early Christian writer for not cataloging events in order.[6]

---

[4] Kenneth Barker, ed., *The NIV Study Bible* (Grand Rapids, MI: Zondervan, 1985), 1437. One precise mathematical comparison puts 53% of Mark in Luke, while in Matthew the total rises to 91% of Mark.

[5] Luke Timothy Johnson, "Book of Luke-Acts," in David Noel Freedman, ed., *The Anchor Bible Dictionary* (New York, NY: Doubleday, 1992), vol. 4, 402–20. Johnson notes how Matthew and Luke seem to spy the same need for clarifications in certain passages in Mark but each makes different verbal adjustments.

[6] Bishop and author Papias of Hierapolis in today's Turkey (AD 60–130) is excerpted by later Christian writers Irenaeus of Lyon (c. AD 180) and

While Matthew and Luke incorporate large portions of Mark, they also seem to draw from another common source. Scholars have observed that in the parts of their books not from Mark, the two writers have material in common (such as "the Lord's prayer," in Mt 6:9–13; Lk 11:2–4, and the "beatitudes," in Mt 5:3-12; Lk 6:20–23). Conceivably, this presumed, interpolated document that they must have accessed could one day be found. More likely, it is lost to history. Scholars primarily in Germany saw the overlap and developed this hypothesis.[7] For lack of a better term, they called this deduced document *"quelle,"* the German word for source, or "Q" for short. Just as Matthew and Luke pulled from Mark, they also drew from Q for their gospel accounts. This interpolated Q collection appears to contain mainly a set of teachings from Jesus; it does not appear to have covered events in the resurrection narrative.

Further investigation into Matthew and Luke shows that each writer also included material *neither* from Mark nor from Q. There is unique material to Matthew (such as the tomb guards in Mt 27:62–66, 28:15) and unique material to Luke (such as the parables of the Good Samaritan and Prodigal Son, Lk 10:29–37, 15:11–32). Unique material to Matthew is sometimes labeled the "M" source, likewise material unique to Luke is called the "L" source. Both Matthew and Luke add weight to the resurrection narrative with

---

Eusebius of Caesarea (c. AD 320) in *Church History,* 3.39.15. Papias quotes another Christian leader, John the Elder, as saying Mark was Peter's interpreter, writing things down accurately, but in no particular order. He says Peter did not concern himself with getting the order straight either. See "Papias of Hierapolis," wikipedia.org.

[7] Scholars in Germany (in the 1830s to 1890s) credited with perceiving the probable existence of the Q document include Friedrich Schleiermacher, Christian Hermann Weisse, Heinrich Julius Holtzmann, and Johannes Weiss. Two British scholars bracketing the Germans, Herbert Marsh (c. 1801) and Burnett Hillman Streeter (c. 1924), wrote treatises that contributed to the Q hypothesis. The hypothesis has come under some serious questioning in recent years. However, this does not change the case for Mark writing first, then Luke and Matthew borrowing substantial portions from Mark.

their unique sources, especially in the appearance accounts that are different from each other (though they are complementary not contradictory, see chapter 2). These accounts likely came to them through their own independent research with witnesses or through other unknown writings.

We need to take into account that in first-century Mediterranean culture communications were mainly done orally. Most of the NT books were read aloud to the gathered believers. Reading and writing (literacy) were not common skills. Due to its emphasis on Torah and synagogue learning, Jewish culture had somewhat higher literacy rates than other ethnic groups. It is conceivable that the original disciples of Jesus did attend synagogue schools and learn to read and write. Yet even when people had learned to read, there were not many published works. Writing was a technical skill. All documents had to be copied by hand, on scrolls or papyrus. Scrolls were highly valued and often kept under lock and key, not available to the common person. Scribes were employed as professionals who could make copies or compose letters. There was no typing, photocopying, emailing or texting, or even printing, apart from handwriting. Written records were kept most commonly for purposes of government and business. Biographies were relatively rare, except for major government and military figures.

What the culture lacked in publishing, it tended to make up in memorizing. People would pass on sayings and stories. These would be carefully committed to memory and in turn passed on to others in very similar form. Among those who followed a teacher or rabbi, the process of memorization was intensified. Disciples were expected to memorize the key utterances of their mentor. As a result, witness reports of events and sayings are much more reliable over time in a culture that prizes committing phrases to memory.[8] Moreover, in the case of the disciples turned apostles, they preached for decades what they had learned from Jesus. Repeating the same message orally locks in the meaning.

---

[8] Richard Bauckham, *Jesus and the Eyewitnesses* (Grand Rapids, MI: Wm. B. Eerdmans, 2006), 240–89.

When it came time to research and write accounts, the NT writers could rely on these long and replenished memories among firsthand and secondhand witnesses.[9]

All these factors give us a sense of how the authors of the gospels worked. They had access to eyewitnesses they could interview or listen to as teachers. They had collections of Jesus's teachings or sayings or parables (gathered from the disciples or people who would listen to Jesus teach in Jerusalem or Galilee). Later, they had full-fledged gospel narratives like the early account of Mark.

Mark's Gospel: Action-Packed, Shortest, Widest Distribution

Mark's gospel is the shortest. It favors episodic action, with transitions linked 47 times by the simple Greek term translated as "immediately" or "quickly" or "just then."[10] Scholars debate whether the author credited with the gospel of Mark is the same John Mark figure active in a number of NT episodes. A key later generation Christian asserts that he is one and the same. He also reports that Mark's major source was the apostle Peter himself.[11] We might imagine the book almost as the gospel of Peter, as told to Mark.[12] Apparently Peter conveyed his memoirs and preaching notes to Mark.[13]

This scenario of Peter sharing his notes with Mark is

---

[9] See Brant Pitre, *The Case for Jesus* (New York, NY: Image, 2016), 85–89.

[10] Several verses in Mark that exemplify this rapid transition factor arise in just the first chapter: Mk 1:12, 18, 20, 23, 28–29, 42–43. See Barker, ed., *NIV Study Bible*, 1493, in the note on Mk 1:12.

[11] See earlier footnote 6 on Papias.

[12] An ancient work called the Gospel of Peter was not included in the canon due to spurious content with Gnostic tendencies and a date of composition later than the first century. See page 51 in the section on sources not selected later in this resource.

[13] Bauckham, *Eyewitnesses*, 155–81. Richard Bauckham expertly argues for Peter's content influence using the gospel's internal evidence: grammatical constructions, point of view, self-deprecation and transparency, all framed by Mark's emphasis on transformation and discipleship.

manifestly reasonable, given what we know about Mark elsewhere in the NT. Peter mentions in a letter that Mark is with him, using the endearing term *"my son"* (1 Pet. 5:13). Years earlier, when Peter escapes from prison, he heads directly to Mark's house in Jerusalem. The house is owned by Mark's mother, named Mary. It is large enough to require servants and to hold *"many people"* gathered for prayer (Acts 12:12). Coming from an affluent family based in Jerusalem, Mark likely spoke Greek, in addition to Aramaic. Historically, Mark's gospel received the widest distribution and fastest acceptance in the early centuries. This likely was due to its association with Peter. Also it may be due to where they eventually resided. Later, both Peter and Mark reportedly lived in Rome, the seat of the empire and the central node for its communications networks.[14] Their collaboration would have occurred before the traditionally reported date of Peter's death in AD 64, though Mark could have written or edited further after his major source's death. The cluelessness of the disciples in Mark's gospel may stem from the humility and self-deprecation typical of Peter. Moreover, the gospel emphasizes the sufferings of Jesus (Mk 8:34–36, 10:45). This may result from the intent of Peter and Mark to prepare the believers in Rome and other cities for the persecution they accurately anticipated was soon to come.

Matthew's Gospel: Adds Jewish Dimensions

Matthew does not say anything in the book about the process of its author, as Luke does. From the content, however, we can tell that a major part of his intention is to convince Jewish people

---

[14] *"Babylon"* in Peter's letter is almost certainly a euphemism for Rome (1 Pet. 5:13). Other later sources support that Peter and Mark were collaborating in Rome: Clement of Alexandria (AD 150-215), Origen (AD 185-254) and Eusebius of Caesarea (AD 260-339), along with the Muratorian Fragment (c. AD 170), the first major list of NT books. See J. Warner Wallace, "Is Mark's Gospel an Early Memoir of the Apostle Peter?" coldcasechristianity.com, 17 Jan 2014.

that Jesus is the Messiah, predicted in the Old Testament. All the other gospels include allusions to OT predictions, but Matthew includes the highest quantity. He seems to view Jesus as "a new Moses," only vastly superior. Like Moses, he forms a new people. Scholars have detected an underlying pattern in the gospel that oscillates from narrative to teaching discourses in five distinct loops (chapters 1–4/5-7; 7–9/10; 11–12/13; 14–17/18; 19–23/24–25).[15] Then the final passion narrative is capped off with Jesus issuing "the Great Commission" (Mt 28:16–20). Certain scholars speculate that this design intentionally imitates the Torah credited to Moses (the first five books of the OT, also known by the Greek term, "the Pentateuch"). After Jerusalem, Antioch in Syria was the largest community of believing Jews. It is a city where Peter frequently visits, and where Paul bases his missionary program. The gospel of Matthew circulates first in this milieu, which makes sense. Its Jewish allusions would be highly relevant to people who knew their Old Testament.

Matthew incorporates even more of Mark than Luke does. More than three quarters of Mark's material appears in Matthew, but Matthew also draws from the Q collection and from still other sources unique to his gospel. Whether the author is the original disciple listed among the twelve in the first three gospels remains a matter of debate. The heavy borrowing from Mark, including the incident when Jesus calls Matthew (also known as Levi) to be his disciple, leads some scholars to question if Matthew the disciple is the writer who puts pen to papyrus (Mk 2:14; Mt 9:9). On the other hand, he could have mentored the writer in Antioch and provided source material beyond Mark and Q; or perhaps he may have funded the project as a relatively affluent ex-tax collector. Hence the gospel might have good reason to bear his name. Yet these associations are speculations. Next to the author of Hebrews, Matthew remains perhaps the most enigmatic major NT author.

---

[15] John P. Meier, "Gospel of Matthew," in Freedman, ed., *Anchor Bible Dictionary*, vol. 4, 627–35.

Luke's Gospel: Emphasizes Outreach to Non-Jews

We have seen how Luke reveals more directly than the other writers how he went about researching his gospel. As for his main content emphases as an author, first he contrasts the acceptance of Jesus by the common people with the rejection of Jesus by the religious elites. One example comes amid the crucifixion account. While the rulers *"sneered at him,"* regular people *"beat their breasts,"* stricken with grief (Lk 23:35, 48).[16] A second emphasis is that Jesus brings salvation to Gentiles, not just to Jews. Luke stresses that faith in Jesus is inclusive not exclusive. The OT figure of Abraham, the father of the Jewish nation, takes a bigger role in Luke's mind (Lk 19:9-10; Acts 3:25, 7:8, 13:26). The blessing of Abraham is passed through the Jewish Messiah Jesus to Gentiles of every nation. Thirdly, Luke emphasizes that the rich should share with the poor (Lk 12:21, 14:12-14, 18:18-27, 18:24-25). A fourth emphasis is on the way the Holy Spirit empowers Jesus, who then sends the Spirit to empower the new people of God for their mission (Lk 3:22, 4:1, 4:14, 10:21, 11:13, 12:12; Acts 1:5-8). Luke sees the continuity between the ministry of Jesus and the mission of the apostles in gathering people into the church—that is, the faith community of Jesus—through the Spirit he sends upon them.

In terms of style, Luke owns the best Greek among the NT writers. He also wears the mantle of the master storyteller. He shows this by the way he records two dozen parables from Jesus in the gospels, and by his journalistic reporting on incidents involving Peter and Paul in the book of Acts. His report of a sea voyage with a shipwreck ranks as one of the most detailed and accurate nautical accounts in ancient Near Eastern literature (Acts 27:1-28:14).

---

[16] Luke Timothy Johnson, "Book of Luke-Acts," in Freedman, ed., *Anchor Bible Dictionary,* vol. 4, 414.

John's Gospel: Cuts Its Own Independent Swath

The book of John is abundantly clear about its purpose.

> *Jesus performed many other signs in the presence of his disciples, which are not recorded in this book. But these are written that you may believe that Jesus is the Messiah, the Son of God, and that by believing you may have life in his name. (John 20:30–31)*

John is not simply informing people about Jesus as a country teacher with a loving disposition and high moral standards. John hopes to persuade them to *believe* in Jesus—as both the long-awaited Jewish Messiah, and as God in human form dwelling or literally *"tabernacling"* with humans in order to bring them a new kind of life (Jn 1:14). The gospel uses the word *"believe"* 98 times and the word *"life"* 36 times.[17] The word *"life"* is often described as *"eternal life."* Its meaning for John seems to correlate with the idea of entering and belonging to *"the kingdom of God"* (in Mark, Luke, Matthew), or to *"the kingdom of heaven"* (in Matthew only). The way John uses it includes not only the sense of life *after* death, but it also means a *quality* of life connected to God that begins when one believes in Jesus. Jesus identifies himself at one point saying, *"I am the resurrection and the life"* and later, *"I am the way, the truth and the life"* (Jn 11:25, 14:6). One is *"born again"* into this new life of connection with God (Jn 1:1–14, 3:1–17). To offer people this eternal quality of life is why Jesus came, and why Jesus died, according to John. He encapsulates this divine purpose and promise in what is probably the most quoted verse in the entire Bible.

> *For God so loved the world, that he gave his one and only Son, that whoever believes in him shall not perish but have eternal life. (John 3:16)*

In John's version, in contrast to Mark's, there is no real effort

---

[17] Barker, ed., *NIV Study Bible*, 1593.

to keep Jesus's identity as Messiah secret. Jesus is clear with his disciples and his opponents from the outset that he is sent from God the Father (Jn 1:48–51). He is in close communion with the Father, doing his work, giving spiritual life to whomever believes (Jn 5:19–30). Later in the week before his death, Jesus assures his disciples as a result of his action they will receive from the Father the gift of the Holy Spirit (also known as their "Advocate") who will be not just *"with you"* but *"in you"* (Jn 14:16–17, 26).

This set of beliefs about God, which scholars term "theology," as expressed in the book of John, once was ruled out of the first century as far too advanced. Referring to Jesus as *"the Word,"* or *"Logos,"* sounded like later Greek philosophy, as did the concept of a god coming to earth in human form, or "incarnation." Placing the writing into the second or third century AD cut off the book from its ostensible author, the disciple John. Now, the consensus for dating the book has shifted back to the first century as a result of two key findings: fragments of early manuscript copies in Egypt, and the collection of OT and other Jewish documents known as the Dead Sea Scrolls.[18] These latter scrolls, preserved in clay jars by a community in the region of Qumran show a pronounced Greek (or Hellenic) influence in the time frame of

---

[18] The oldest known manuscript from the NT is actually a fragment found of the gospel of John. It narrates part of the interrogation of Jesus by the Roman governor Pilate (Jn 18:31–33, 37–38). It was found in 1920 in Egypt and brought to the John P. Rylands Library in Manchester, England, where it remains. It is known by the number "p52" and usually is dated between AD 125–150. To have been copied, transported, and used in Egypt far from John's presumed later base in Ephesus, it originally would have been written in the first century, most scholars now agree. (See "p52: A fragment of the Gospel of John," kchanson.com, 7 Jun 2004.) The Dead Sea scrolls contain parts of all books of the OT except Esther (probably due to the overt sexuality in that book without a direct mention of God). The scrolls include as well many writings on Jewish theology and practice with Hellenistic accents, similar to the philosophical approach in John. All these writings are dated between 150 BC and AD 70. That range places them either prior to or within the lifetime of the disciple John; it validates his or his collaborator's mode of expression within the first century. See more on the Dead Sea Scrolls in the Found in the Ground Index, 9.1.

150 BC to AD 70. The early Christians Irenaeus, Tertullian, and Clement of Alexandria had vouched for John as the author, so this shift correlated with their earlier assertions.[19] Amazing to some naysayers, John the disciple very well could be the source for the gospel that traditionally bears his name after all.

Like Jesus, John was from Galilee. He and his brother James worked in their father's commercial fishing business. They seem to have had fiery tempers and high ambitions (Mk 3:17, 10:35–45). The family were partners in their fishing business with the leader of the disciples, Peter. These three men Jesus selected to form his inner circle. They were the ones who took the epic hike with Jesus up a mountain in northern Israel where he underwent a transfiguration that left a lasting impact on them (Mk 9:2–10, see chapter 3). Peter definitely and John probably in later letters refer to this mountaineering experience (2 Pet. 1:16; 1 Jn 1:1). John and Peter, partners in business and ministry, often show up together as a pair of evangelists, teachers and leaders (Jn 20:3–10; Acts 3:1–11, 4:1–19, 8:14–25).

Tradition holds John lived the longest of the original disciples, probably into his 90s. That longevity allows his gospel to be dated after the others, although still in the first century. Interestingly, among the four gospels, only the gospel of John never refers by name to the disciple John (nor to his brother James, nor to his mother Salome, but only to him as one of the sons of Zebedee, his father, in Jn 21:2, see chapter 1). Instead, in episodes in John's gospel he is called either *"the other disciple"* (Jn 18:16, 20:2–4, 8), or famously*"the disciple whom Jesus loved"* (Jn 13:23, 19:26, 20:2, 21:7, 21:20). Is it humility, or is it seemingly the opposite, a point of pride, or is there some other concealed literary reason? We do not know, but it certainly identifies the book more closely with the original, inner-circle disciple. To be sure, the book itself indicates that there is a writer involved who most probably is not the actual beloved disciple (Jn 19:35, 21:24). This writer credits the beloved disciple with eyewitness testimony that stands behind the written gospel. Some scholars

---

[19] Eusebius, *Church History* 6.14.7.

think that this writer was a disciple of John, or alternatively that he was a contemporary outside the twelve disciples but still part of the larger entourage of Jesus followers who also had personal contact with Jesus. John the disciple may have enlisted a scribe to write and structure his recollections; or he may have given witness in teachings, and in some written notes, that were formulated into a larger, highly literary work by a person in his community with facility in the Greek language. Neither scribal help nor a follower who writes from John's teachings, memoirs or notes would discredit John as the primary source for the book.[20]

In recent years, scholars have noted how the gospel of John shows strong knowledge of Jewish life in the first century. The author knows Jewish geography, citing Cana near Jesus's hometown, and noting Bethany is less than two miles/three km from Jerusalem (Jn 2:1, 11:18, 21:2). He knows Jewish customs and trial procedures (Jn 18:19–40, 19:31, 40). He grasps details of the layout of Jerusalem, like the Pool of Siloam, long thought to be invented, but an excavation vindicated the account in 2004.[21] Like Matthew, John brings up Jewish prophecies he sees being fulfilled by Jesus, especially at the site of the cross (Jn 12:14–16, 19:23–24, 28–29, 36–37). Details of descriptions of specific incidents bear the marks of eyewitness reports (Jn 19:33–35, 20:2–10).

To be sure, the book of John displays some marked differences with the other gospels in the order of Jesus's ministry and in

---

[20] Being assisted by a scribe was common in those times, especially when Greek was a second language for the writer. The disciples, like Jesus, spoke Aramaic, although the synagogue readings were spoken from the Hebrew bible. Peter makes a point of crediting his partner in ministry Silas for helping him write his first letter (1 Pet. 5:12). See section on the letters of Peter later in this resource. Also, the way Mark structured notes from Peter's preaching to compile his gospel may be similar to the way the writer of the gospel of John, conjectured by some scholars, worked from John's teachings and reminiscences. See upcoming discussion on 1 John for one possible collaborator in the writing of John's gospel.

[21] The Pool of Siloam was identified by Ronny Reich and Eli Shukron in 2004. See Found in the Ground Index, 3.3.

the more philosophical way he teaches. It nevertheless follows the sequence of the resurrection events similarly through trial, crucifixion, burial, and appearances.

Yet John adds significant details within the overall parameters established by the other three gospels. For the scenes at the night trial, he knows the layout of the high priest's house (Jn 18:15–16). For the trial of Jesus before the Roman governor, John identifies the precise location as a broad stone pavement, noting the Aramaic word for it (Jn 19:13). Excavations have pinpointed this site convincingly.[22] At the cross, John's gospel includes Mary the mother of Jesus among the women who are grieving. At some point John, alone among the disciples (assuming he is the beloved disciple), comes to the execution site. From his precarious vantage point on the cross before he dies, Jesus asks John to take care of his mother (Jn 19:26–27). At the burial, the gospel's account includes a second council member at the scene, Nicodemus. At the tomb, it adds an apostolic footrace between the beloved disciple and Peter (Jn 20:3–10). It covers very personal dialogs with the risen Jesus involving Mary Magdalene, and later, Thomas the disciple. Providing a tremendous crescendo to the gospel is the outburst of Thomas after he is invited by Jesus to touch his hands and side: *"My Lord and My God"* (Jn 20:24–29). Catalyzing such confident belief is what John sets out as his purpose in the gospel (Jn 20:30–31).[23]

---

[22] The site of Herod's palace was found in Jerusalem in 1943, then in 2000 underwent extensive re-digging. The palace sat on an elevated platform on the west side of the upper city. It was an early project by Herod of flattening and enlarging a plaza; it was followed later by the more ambitious program to enlarge the temple mount complex. The site matches the description in Josephus of Roman governors judging on the pavement outside the palace (*War* 2.14.8); it fits with John's reference to *"gabbatha,"* an Aramaic term meaning *"stone pavement"* (in Greek *"lithostraton"*). The finding supports the detailed account of the trial scene as recounted in John (Jn 18:28, 19:8–9, 13–16). See Found in the Ground Index, 3.6.

[23] A later appearance featuring Peter and John with other disciples beside the Sea of Galilee finishes the book. First, it verifies that Peter is fully restored by Jesus after his grievous denials. Secondly, it clarifies that

Of the four gospels, the gospel of John is the outlier, the one most different from the others. Unlike Matthew and Luke, it does not depend in any respect on Mark, nor does it include the material from the hypothesized Q source. Given our purpose to evaluate the probability of the resurrection narratives, its status as an *independent source* to examine in parallel with Mark's gospel is nothing less than, for lack of a better word, "a godsend."

Gospels: Demonstrate Access to Eyewitnesses

To recap, even though this assessment of the gospels as individual sources is brief, it shows their strengths. They claim to work from eyewitness material. Among the gospels, John appears to be written at least in part by the disciple himself, and he personally vouches for the content (Jn 19:35, 21:24). Luke acknowledges that he himself is not an eyewitness, but he has received what some of the original disciples and teachers (and others in his well-connected circle) have handed down to him. With its fast-moving action connected by simple transitions and few teaching sections, Mark reflects the memoirs and preaching of Peter. Matthew may well have been the other disciple to write a gospel himself; or the gospel may have come from a later disciple he mentored in some way in a community of believing Jews, most probably in Antioch, Syria.[24]

Jesus never said John would not die before he returns, as rumor had it. These appear to be appended somewhat after the original gospel endpoint. Unlike the situation with the ending of Mark's gospel (see chapter 2), the added section seems to continue in the same style as the original writing. For an intriguing argument that this final section is not added on but stands as an integral conclusion to the gospel, see Bauckham, *Eyewitnesses*, 363–69.

[24] Antioch was home to a large community of Jews, many of them believers. Due to relatively tolerant religious laws, they could practice their faith freely and still retain status as full citizens.

Gospel Sequel Narrates Apostolic Adventures

Beyond the four gospels, we have another key historical source. This source covers the ground of what happens over the thirty years after Jesus departs. It records the actions taken by certain resurrection witnesses and other believers and what happens to them. Our quest to find historical evidence that affects the probability of the resurrection event is powerfully enhanced by investigating how witnesses and believers operate in the succeeding years (see the lines of evidence in chapters 4–8).

The gospels basically stop with Jesus's appearances after he rises from the dead. (As has been noted, our manuscript of Mark stops even earlier, with the mystified women rushing away from the empty tomb.) In fact only one gospel writer, Luke, narrates the life of Jesus all the way to his leaving the earth, commonly known as "the Ascension."[25] Still, the account is brief and ends abruptly. Luke's gospel account can give the impression that Jesus leaves earth quickly, maybe the same day or the day after the resurrection occurs (Lk 24:49–53).

Lucky for us Luke does not stop his history writing there. He writes a sequel to his gospel in the book of Acts. We know it is Luke writing again although his name is not mentioned as the author. The author writes to the same person who is the patron of his first book, Theophilus. The style of the Greek language bears Luke's characteristic sophisticated mode. Early Christian sources attribute Acts to Luke (the Muratorian Canon; also Eusebius, *Church History* 3.4). At one point, the author himself joins Paul on a missionary journey through Greece and he starts to use the pronoun *"we"* to describe their travels (Acts 16:10). Paul's letters confirm that Luke was one of his treasured companions (Philemon 24; also Col. 4:14; 2 Tim. 4:11).[26] With his two lengthy books, Luke ends up writing nearly one quarter of the entire New

---

[25] John does not narrate the ascension, but indicates it is coming up in the near future (Jn 6:62, 20:17).

[26] As noted before, the latter two (Colossians, 2 Timothy) remain disputed by some critics as not written by Paul himself, but even (on the outside

Testament, more by volume than any of the other nine or so NT authors.[27] Luke begins his sequel in this manner.

> *In my former book, Theophilus, I wrote about all that Jesus began to do and to teach until the day he was taken up to heaven, after giving instructions through the Holy Spirit to the apostles he had chosen. After his suffering, he presented himself to them and gave many convincing proofs that he was alive. He appeared to them over a period of forty days and spoke about the kingdom of God. (Acts 1:1–3)*

One advantage of a sequel is that the author can make clarifications. Here Luke records the important report that Jesus does not leave shortly after he rises, but he roams in Galilee and Jerusalem for more than a month. That allows sufficient time for all the recorded appearances to occur (see chapter 2). It also allows time for Jesus to teach the disciples how the writings in the OT predicted his death and resurrection (see chapter 9).

---

chance) if so they are probably from persons in Paul's circle and likely would offer accurate information on Luke.

[27] The consensus set of NT authors includes at a minimum these nine or ten: Matthew, Mark, Luke, John and/or his collaborator, Paul, the unknown author of Hebrews, James, Peter and Jude. Some scholars expand the list by challenging that some letters bearing the names of Paul, Peter and John were actually written by others. To be sure, Paul wrote jointly with Silas and Timothy in his two letters to the Thessalonians, so we could add those two names. Peter had help from Silas as well on his first letter. See more on the letters of Peter and John following in this resource. Either way, Paul would still hold the record for the most individual writings included in the NT, with at least seven, and conceivably thirteen. By page volume, Luke leads the NT authorial pack with his comprehensive gospel and his lengthy narrative of the apostolic outreach in Acts, amounting to about one quarter of the total writing in the NT.

Book of Acts: Speeches Have Traceable Sources, Fit the Era

Mass communication in the first century relied on orally delivered in-person speeches. So it is natural that the apostles are depicted frequently giving speeches about their faith to diverse audiences, including ruling councils and kings. Speeches placed into narratives are common in Greco-Roman historical writing. It is possible Luke is present with Paul at his later speeches. For the earlier ones Paul probably summarized them for Luke. As for Peter's speeches, Luke was a colleague with Mark in Paul's entourage, and Mark likely shared the memoirs or notes he had received from Peter.

The longest recorded speech in Acts comes from Stephen, an early Greek-speaking believer in Jerusalem (see chapter 5). It is harder to tell how Luke received that speech content. Paul in his prior life as a persecutor of believers was on the scene, and might have recalled the content. Philip the Evangelist (not the original disciple) was appointed alongside Stephen as a deacon, so he might have accompanied Stephen to his tragic hearing before the Sanhedrin (Acts 6:5, 7:1–60, see also chapters 5 and 9). Decades later Luke and Paul were in close enough contact with Philip to stay as his guests on their way to Jerusalem (Acts 21:8). These interactions among Luke's possible sources buffer him against the pedestrian accusation that he completely makes up the speech content from scratch. Certainly the quotations in the accounts are excerpts from speeches that ran longer. It also would not be true to the time to expect word-for-word transmission of these speeches. Rather the content and general flow of thought presented in that historical moment is what reasonably would have been preserved.[28]

---

[28] For a full discussion of speeches in Acts, see F.F. Bruce, *The Speeches in the Acts of the Apostle* (London, UK: The Tyndale Press, 1942), 5–27, biblicalstudies.org.uk. Three decades later, Bruce revisited his essay in a "festschrift" or publication to honor a fellow scholar. See F.F. Bruce, "The Speeches in Acts—Thirty Years After," Robert Banks, ed., *Reconciliation and Hope. New Testament Essays on Atonement and Eschatology Presented to L.L. Morris on his 60th Birthday,* (Carlisle, UK: The Paternoster Press, 1974), 53–68. Also available at biblicalstudies.org.uk.

Acts: Recounts Challenges, Motivates Believers

Luke does not state his purposes overtly in writing Acts, but the material he includes reveals at least some of them.[29] First, he wants to show how the apostles fulfilled their mission given to them by Jesus to be his witnesses, *"from Jerusalem, Judea, Samaria, and to the ends of the earth"* (Acts 1:8). He portrays scenes of Peter and Stephen in Jerusalem, Peter in Judea, Philip (the Evangelist) in Samaria, with Paul taking the gospel from Antioch around the northern Mediterranean world through *"Asia"* (today's Turkey), then throughout Greece and eventually to Rome. Perhaps the reason he ends with Paul in prison and his fate up for grabs is because the focus is on the mission, not the person; therefore, it is enough to end with the mission accomplished (see alternative explanations for the abrupt end of Acts in resource 2).

Second, Luke demonstrates how the message adapts and engages with diverse cultures, reaching both Jews and the diverse Gentile societies (Acts 4:8–12, 13:16–26, 17:16–34). Scholars observe that Luke modulates his language to fit the culture he describes. At times, he uses Aramaic terms when the action is set in Israel and when the scene changes he drops them for Greek idioms.[30]

Third, Luke shows the power of the message and the persistence of the messengers when running up against persecution. To see the resilient apostles get hit hard and yet succeed in their mission would be encouraging to future generations of Christians, many of whom would face equally vicious opposition. Hearing these accounts might motivate them like their forebears to trust the Holy Spirit to comfort and empower them.

Finally, Luke takes pains to show the differences and rifts that occur between believers (Paul and Barnabas over Mark, Acts 15:37–40; Paul and James over keeping the law, Acts 15:1–29). Some of these differences are resolved in the scope of the book and

---

[29] This discussion owes much to Barker, ed., *NIV Study Bible*, 1642, with contributor credit to Lewis Foster.

[30] Luke Timothy Johnson, "Book of Luke-Acts," in Freedman, ed., *Anchor Bible Dictionary*, vol. 4, 408–9.

some are not. It demonstrates to future believers to try to work out their differences, but always to keep in mind the paramount mission must go on. There are plenty of places in the world to seek out new tribes and ethnicities and populations in order to be witnesses of the life-saving message of Jesus.

First/Second Peter: Scribes Differ, Same Heart

In the gospels, Peter serves as the leader of the disciples and the right hand man of Jesus. He runs a fishing business on the sea of Galilee with his brother Andrew, and with the family of the brothers James and John. Those two brothers and Peter form the inner circle of the disciples of Jesus (see chapter 3). Jesus changes his original name "Simon" to "Peter," translated in English as "Rock" or perhaps "Rocky"(Jn 1:42; Mt 16:18). Peter likely possesses a personal magnetism that makes him a natural leader of other people (see chapter 4). Peter is action-oriented, sometimes overly impulsive but nearly always seeking to follow the lead of Jesus. He is crushed when he denies his friendship with Jesus at the crucial moment when Jesus is under arrest (see prelude for chapter 4). Yet he heals and recovers once Jesus appears to him individually and counsels him personally after the resurrection (Lk 24:34, Jn 21:15–19, see chapter 2). He steps out as the movement's first evangelist, courageously speaking to crowds or authorities when they arrest him (see chapter 4). He builds up other churches in Antioch and Samaria from his base in Jerusalem, where he remains (after Jesus departs) for at least twenty years before relocating to Rome. He eventually dies there as a martyr in a wave of persecution in about AD 64. Most scholars credit him as the main source for the gospel of Mark as we saw earlier.

Two letters in the NT are attributed to Peter. Some scholars balk at these attributions. Regarding the first letter, they say the Greek is *too good* for Peter to be writing. It is smooth and idiomatic. A Galilean fisherman would not have this kind of Greek vocabulary. However, this is not hard to explain. Peter likely had a smattering of business Greek to successfully negotiate prices and materials for his fishing business, but probably he did need help writing. In fact, he mentions who helps him, namely Silas (1 Pet. 5:12).

Not to be dissuaded, the more dismissive scholars assign Silas as simply the letter carrier for Peter, not his co-writer or collaborator. This theory pointedly ignores the NT evidence for the verbal talents of Silas. After the epic Jerusalem council when circumcision is waived for new believers, the council members entrust Silas to take their letter of record to the next largest community of believers in Antioch. They do not send him solely as a postal messenger, but to *"confirm by word of mouth what we are writing"* (Acts 15:27). Clearly, Silas is a *verbal* person. In Antioch, he is a leader and prophet who *"said much"* (Acts 15:22, 32). Years before he helps Peter write, Silas writes with Paul and Timothy to the Thessalonians, twice (1 Thess. 1:1, 2 Thess. 1:1). Paul himself, no slouch at writing letters with his advanced education, receives help writing Romans from another assistant, Tertius (Rom. 16:22). In 2 Thess. 3:17, Paul notes he writes his final word *"in my own hand,"* implying someone else wrote down the preceding text, probably Silas.

A second objection to Peter's authorship comes from the theory that his emphasis on suffering as a believer reflects a later time period in the AD 90s under the later Roman Emperor, Domitian. This again is easy to explain. Peter himself perishes in the earlier persecution under the emperor Nero in the AD 60s. It is not hard to imagine that Peter foresaw the antagonism building and coming to an eventual crisis, and wanted to prepare his fellow believers. Suffering is not all for naught, Peter assures them. They can endure it because the example of Jesus shows God will triumph, because he guarantees the inheritance he has laid up for them in heaven (1 Pet. 1:4), and because Jesus will return in power (1 Pet. 1:13). Peter is emotionally moved by reflecting on the atoning sacrifice of Jesus as described in Isaiah 53 (see chapter 9). You can hear him speaking from his own experience when he quotes the truth he had absorbed from being forgiven and restored by Jesus. He echoes Isaiah 53:5 as he writes to the scattered yet chosen exiles: *"by his wounds you have been healed"* (1 Pet. 1:1–2, 2:24).

There is no compelling reason not to date the letter before Peter's death. Because he refers to letters by Paul, most written in the AD 50s though later ones possibly in the early 60s, the letter would not be dated earlier than the later 50s. Probably it would be written in the early 60s, and probably from Rome (1 Pet. 3:15–16, 5:13). Confirming this view that the letter comes from Peter are the usual suspects of later-generation Christian writers, including Polycarp, Clement of Rome, Irenaeus, Tertullian, Clement of Alexandria and Origen.

As for the second letter attributed to Peter, some scholars claim it cannot be from Peter because the Greek is *not as good* as the first letter. As we saw, Peter had help with the first letter from Silas, who helped Paul on letters as well. Silas does not seem to be present for this letter. So Peter probably is using the services of a less cogent scribe or maybe he is in a do-it-yourself mode. Either way, that explains the difference in the Greek. Next, the observation that there is borrowing between 2 Pet. 2:1–19 and Jude 4–18 does not preclude Peter from writing it. Borrowing was common, as shown by the gospel writers Matthew and Luke, who without attribution borrow freely (from Mark and probably Q). Also, note another objection to Peter's authorship. The heresies and false teachers that the letter condemns are assigned by some scholars to a later century; but they could just as well have been developing in the first century. Finally, the personal touches also bespeak Peter as the source for the letter. Early on he says *"we did not follow cleverly devised stories when we told you about the coming of our Lord Jesus Christ in power, but we were eyewitnesses of his majesty"* (2 Pet. 1:16). He asserts that the origin of Scripture comes from God, that *"men spoke from God as they were carried along by the Holy Spirit."* He employs the Greek term for *"carried along,"* commonly used to describe a boat being borne by the wind, a word Peter the fisherman uses six times in his two letters (2 Pet. 1:21).[31] He also famously speaks of the hope of *"a new heaven and a new earth, where righteousness dwells"* that surfaces after the meltdown of the old order (2 Pet. 3:11–13). Then in an aside, he refers to his earlier letter (2 Pet. 3:1). In Greek style, the second letter differs from the first, but in content there are enough indicators to credit both letters to Peter.

First John: The Letter Sounds Just Like the Gospel of John

Few scholars deny that the first letter of John in the NT is written by the same person who wrote the gospel of John. (Likewise the second and third letters generally, despite some skeptics, are ascribed to the same person. However, these are not included in our historical investigation.) Scholars may argue over who wrote the gospel of John, but most agree that whoever wrote John also wrote the first letter of John. The similarities in vocabulary and in the simple, defiant writing style are too great to ignore. The use of dualities in the letter are almost identical to those in the gospel: life/death, light/darkness, truth/lies, love/ hate. As in the gospel, the writer of the letter claims to be an eyewitness.[32] In case anyone misses this fact, he tells them at the outset in multiple phrases.

---

[31] For more on the use of this term, see Mike Ratliff, "Carried Along by the Holy Spirit," mikeratliff.wordpress.com, n.d. Ratliff vividly writes the following: "Peter loved this word. He used it six times in his two epistles. He was a fisherman. He was used to hard work outside in the elements. When he used 'pheromenoi' he was painting a picture of men being moved, motivated, and mastered by the Holy Spirit according to the will of God. This is underscored by the verb tense. Why? Because it is passive, 'holy men,' which (sic) is the subject were being acted upon by the Holy Spirit, and because it is present, this action was continuous. Those 'holy men', therefore, were being 'continually carried along' by the Holy Spirit like a ship is carried along as its sails are filled with the wind to drive it to its destination."

[32] The candidate other than John the disciple of Jesus is usually an early Christian known as John the Elder. He is mentioned in a lost writing (c.

> *That which was from the beginning, which we have heard, which we have seen with our eyes, which we have looked at and our hands have touched—this we proclaim concerning the Word of life. The life appeared; we have seen it and testify to it, and we proclaim to you the eternal life, which was with the Father and has appeared to us. (1 John 1:1–2)*

Another telling clue that John is the one writing is the tone later in the letter. It reveals that he is in advanced age, as he calls the adult recipients of the letter *"dear children"* (1 Jn 2:12, 18, 28, 3:7, 18).

In content, he retraces from his gospel the emphasis on Jesus as the atoning sacrifice for sins (1 Jn 1:7-10, 2:1-2, 4:10). As in the gospel, he stresses the love of God in sending Jesus. Due to God's love, those who receive forgiveness in Jesus also are *"born of God"* (1 Jn 3:9). He asserts that those born of God will start living like children of God, full of love and obedience. They will not live like degenerates or murderers, as if they were children of the evil one (1 Jn 3:7-10, 4:7-12, 5:1-5). John takes aim at a particular heresy that theorizes that Jesus does not really suffer on the cross (1 Jn 4:2). The theory asserts that Jesus was merely a man, but became divine for a bracketed time period. It starts at the moment when he is baptized, when the Divine Spirit comes upon him. However, before he goes to the cross, the Spirit leaves him, and he suffers only as a human.[33] John realizes the heresy negates any

---

110) by Papias, a church leader in Hierapolis, who is quoted by the later church historian, Eusebius. John the Elder is not John the disciple. He may have been a protégé of John the disciple, or possibly a disciple of Jesus who was outside the circle of the twelve original disciples. Some scholars credit him with the letters 2 and 3 John. Other scholars go so far as to credit him with the gospel of John and 1 John. He may have collaborated with John the disciple in some way. Nevertheless, the fourth gospel remains related to the original disciple by the very fact, ironically, that it strangely does not name him or his brother as the other gospels do.

[33] John is confronting what later is called the "Docetic heresy." The term derives from the Greek word "to seem." Basically, the heresy claims that

atoning power for the sins of others, if Jesus does not retain the combination of human and divine natures.

Though fairly brief, the letter packs a punch, replete with famous one-liners. *"God is love"* (1 Jn 4:16). *"We love because he first loved us"* (1 Jn 4:19). *"... everyone born of God overcomes the world"* (1 Jn 5:4). One of his best lines shows John at his most succinct and defiant, yet direct and encouraging. *"Whoever has the Son has life; whoever does not have the Son of God does not have life"* (1 Jn 5:12).

James: Keep the Faith Despite Suffering

Although several persons featured in the NT are named James, this letter almost certainly is written by James, the brother of Jesus. James probably was the oldest brother of Jesus, as he is mentioned first on the sibling list (Mt 13:55). James did not believe in Jesus as the Messiah until after the resurrection (Jn 7:2–5). Along with other family members, he at one point seemed to feel that Jesus was going insane and so he came to take away his socially disruptive brother (Mk 3:31–32). Apparently the personal appearance that Jesus made to him after rising shook James to his core. It likely was the impetus that caused him not only to believe and join the disciples, but also to take up the leadership mantle in the Jerusalem church (1 Cor. 15:7; Acts 1:14, 15:13, 21:18).

James commands great respect. When Peter is rescued from jail and knocks at the house of the family of Mark, he stays only briefly, but asks them to be sure and tell James about his deliverance (Acts

---

Jesus only *seemed* to have a human body, and only *seemed* to suffer on the cross, not in reality. It denies the tension, or paradox, that Jesus could have both human and divine natures. Epidemics of the Docetic heresy in various strains break out primarily in the first four centuries of Christian history. A prominent version that intertwined itself in several early Christian communities is known as the "Gnostic heresy." It imagined an entire narrative construct around a different identity for God the Father and a different mission for Jesus, one of education not salvation. For more angles on the Gnostic heresy, see the list of sources not selected for our investigation, later in this resource, on pages 48–49.

12:17). When the council is called to confront the circumcision issue, James makes the final decision after listening to Peter's input (Acts 15:19–21). Paul also shows respect for James. He shows this several years after converting when he stays two weeks with Peter in Jerusalem and meets James as well on that visit. Then much later after his last missionary journey, Paul makes sure to report back to James in Jerusalem (Gal. 1:19; Acts 21:18). Unlike Peter and John, who Christian tradition asserts eventually leave their base in Jerusalem for Rome and Ephesus respectively, James remains to shepherd the church in Jerusalem. He dies on the job, suffering martyrdom at the hands of a rogue high priest in AD 62, as recorded by Josephus (*Antiquities* 20.9.1, see chapter 5).

The letter of James bears a strong Jewish character, leading some scholars to conclude that it may rival Galatians as the earliest letter in the NT, potentially written as early as AD 50. The greeting *"to the twelve tribes scattered among the nations"* clearly shows that James has Jewish recipients in mind. They may have been chased out of Israel during an early wave of persecution, or they may have migrated. Either way they remain under duress in their current locations. The way James goes about conveying his counsel reflects a strong Jewish sensitivity. Some scholars see correlations with Matthew's version of the sermon on the mount given by Jesus.[34] The tone of the exposition in James also takes after the book of Proverbs. Further, the examples James holds up are heroes of Jewish faith, among them Abraham, Job and Elijah. He also cites Rahab, the former prostitute who believed in the God of Israel and helped the Israelites conquer her city of Jericho (James 2:20–26; Gen. 15:6; Josh. 2:1–21, 6:17, 22–25).

James seems to have at least a twofold purpose in writing to his fellow Jewish believers. First, he wants to fortify their endurance in the face of suffering. He assures them that tough

---

[34] Here are some parallels between the prose of James and Matthew's record of the Sermon on the Mount: James 2:5 with Mt 5:3; James 3:10–12 with Mt 7:15–20; James 3:18 with Mt. 5:9; James 5:2–3 with Mt 6:19–20; James 5:12 with Mt 5:33–37. See Barker, ed., *NIV Study Bible*, 1879–80, with contributor credit to Donald W. Burdick.

times will actually work to create inner strength and fullness of life. Then secondly, he wants to urge them to put their faith into action, and not use God's grace as an excuse to sin.

Hebrews: Author Contends Temple Is Obsolete

After two millennia, the author of Hebrews continues to remain unknown. For centuries, many thought the book was written by the apostle Paul. Few people assert that today. Differences from Paul's established ways include no salutation or author identification; not quoting from the Hebrew OT (Masoretic) but from the Greek OT (Septuagint); and not claiming special revelations, but mentioning that he is taught by other apostles (Heb. 2:3).

The writer expounds with authority and shows exceedingly detailed knowledge of the rituals of the temple and the practices of Judaism. Candidates for the author currently are narrowed down to two persons. One is Apollos, due to his being *"a learned man, with a thorough knowledge of the Scriptures,"* as Luke puts it (Acts 18:24). The other candidate is Barnabas, Paul's original mentor and travel companion. He was in high demand as a teacher in Antioch, and he himself hailed from the tribe of Levi, the priestly line (Acts 4:36, Acts 13:1–4). Some view the letter as addressed to the *"large number of priests"* who overheard the disciples' preaching in the temple precincts and *"became obedient to the faith"* (Acts 6:7). Nonetheless, the content of the letter applies equally well to any Jewish Christian believers who held fast to the temple procedures.

The author obviously writes before the temple destruction of AD 70. A main purpose in writing the document is to unwind the devotion of Jesus believers to the temple system. It would be absurd not to mention that the temple is gone, if that were the case. Plus, the author uses the present tense to refer to the temple, implying it is still standing.

The book declares Jesus as the mediator of a new covenant, as predicted by Jeremiah (Jer. 31:31–34). It is superior to the old covenant delivered under the regime led by Moses and by Aaron, the first high priest (Heb. 3:3, 8:6). The Greek word for *"superior"* occurs fifteen times in the letter.[35] The old covenant was *"a shadow of the good things that are coming—not the realities themselves,"* and could not actually pay for sin and transform the heart (Heb. 10:1-4). The death of Jesus atones for sin. Its effectiveness is verified by the resurrection (Heb. 2:9, 9:28). It opens the pathway to the true temple in heaven, where God is present in his glory. As the Messiah without sin, the writer of Hebrews contends, Jesus has entered into that holy sanctum as both our high priest and as our substitute sacrifice.

> *Unlike the other high priests, he does not need to offer sacrifices day after day, first for his own sins, and then for the sins of the people. He sacrificed for their sins once for all when he offered himself. (Hebrews 7:27)*

In this way Jesus fulfills the promise to Abraham, that all nations would be blessed through him. The author rolls out a hall of fame of faith heroes, in two groups: first, those who early in the Genesis account put their faith in God's creative goodness; then secondly those who believed later in the promise God specifically made to Abraham to form nations and bless the world through his offspring (Gen. 12:7, 13:15-16, 15:5, 22:18). These believers persevered despite long delays and fierce persecution. The author warns his readers to do likewise and to not shrink back from trusting God, but to believe and be saved. They can take comfort in the promise God makes which remains in force, *"Never will I leave you; never will I forsake you"* (Heb. 13:5b, echoing Deut. 31:6, 8).

Josephus: Corroborates NT Accounts, Catalogs Culture

As we saw in the main book prologue, Josephus (AD 37-100) was a major first-century historian, traversing the testy territory of interconnections between Judea and Rome. He was Jewish

---

[35] Barker, ed., *NIV Study Bible*, 1858.

himself. A military official, he had been placed in charge of defending Galilee, the region where Jesus had ministered about thirty-five years earlier. Josephus deserts the Jewish military, once he accurately ascertains that it had no chance of defeating Rome. He lucks out when he makes a prediction that the Roman general, Vespasian, will ascend to the emperor's throne. It happens, and the family name of the emperor "Flavius" is given to Josephus, along with patronage that allows him to research and write his histories. His purpose seems to be to explain the uniqueness of the Jewish people to a Roman audience, not so much to preserve and revel in Jewish history for its own sake. He writes several books, but two are important for our investigation.

First, he writes *The Jewish War*, c. AD 75, only a few years after the actual events. It covers the Jewish rebellion against Rome and the resulting invasion from AD 66–73. About two decades later, Josephus completes another work, *Antiquities of the Jews*. It takes him so long because this book starts at the outset of creation, spanning the history of the Jews along the entire OT in the first ten books. The next ten books cover the period from where the OT leaves off at about 400 BC to the time that the Roman-Jewish war breaks out in AD 66. In places, Josephus decides to put his own spin on the material. For instance, he deletes the golden calf incident in the wilderness, a calamitous point in Israelite history.

In the earlier book *The Jewish War*, Josephus sticks closer to the facts, especially when he himself lived through them. He knew the battles well since he was a Roman operative and eyewitness. He serves as an interpreter for the Romans, hoping in vain to convince the occupants of Jerusalem to surrender without a bloodbath, to no avail. Josephus wrote originally in either Hebrew or Aramaic but most scholars hold that the writings were translated during his lifetime into Greek, the literary language of the era, and later into Latin. He underscores several accounts by Luke in Acts. He provides kaleidoscopic cultural background information on customs, places, social factions, leading figures and major events.

Sources Not Selected for This Resurrection Investigation

Many modern scholars find sources of endless fascination in alternative ancient documents that conflict with the Bible's accounts. These scholarly explorations often attract widespread media attention. Upon closer inspection, these documents, while often entertaining and sensationalized, come loaded with problems that make them historically unreliable.

For two main reasons, this historical investigation of the resurrection of Jesus is not based on these non-canonical documents. First, these are written later than the NT documents selected, all of which now are widely considered to have been written in the first century. The non-selected documents listed below are dated to the second century (AD 100s) or third century (AD 200s). Many more not on this list arrive centuries later, too far from the time of Jesus to be anything but creative invention. Plenty of invention appears already in the earlier-dated alternatives that we will discuss. That is the second reason for excusing these documents from our historical investigation of the resurrection. These writings simply contain self-evident bogus stuff. They just do not bear the seriousness seen in the New Testament. Given below for each document are samples of problems that make it historically questionable.

Three other factors are evident in most of these writings. First, many of these documents are slanted by a religious belief known as "Gnosticism." It helps to pause for a brief definition. Gnosticism is related to the Christian heresy of Docetism. Docetism is the view that Jesus *only seemed* to have a human body, and *only seemed* to suffer on the cross, but not in reality. Indeed, basic Docetism crops up in some of these Gnostic writings. Yet Gnosticism goes way beyond discussions of Jesus's human and divine natures. It creates a whole new imagined narrative, especially in its later forms. Gnosticism asserts that a lower deity, the god of the OT, creates our earth, maliciously. The material world is evil, and our bodies have trapped inside them the divine spark, our true selves. The true, albeit remote, deity wants to liberate us. He sends Jesus as a messenger, not as a savior, with this message of soul liberation. Those who get and accept the knowledge or "gnosis" will be lifted at death to an eternal spiritual realm. Those who do not will remain in the evil earth for a second go round, reincarnated and trapped in another body. Without proper knowledge, they may never make it out. Jesus himself is executed for bringing this teaching, so the Gnostic myth goes, but his spirit or spark leaves his body before he suffers on the cross. This "Christian Gnosticism" is subtle, yet to the early church fathers, radically heretical. *Knowledge* saves you, not the atoning death and triumphal resurrection of Jesus. It denies a major, reverberating message of the OT that the God of Israel is the Creator of all things, captured in repeated phrases like *"I am God and there is no other"* (Deut. 4:35, 39–40; Isa. 44:6–8, 45:5–6, 18–22, 46:9–11; Joel 2:27). It also denies the major NT message that salvation comes from trusting in the work of Jesus, in his death for our sins and in his resurrection victory over death, which opens up to us eternal life (Acts 2:38; Rom. 3:25–26; Isa. 43:10–11, 44:68; 1 Cor. 15:3; 2 Cor. 5:19; 1 Pet. 3:18; Eph. 2:4–10; Col. 2:13–15).

A second tendency in these documents is that they devalue if not outrightly denounce marriage, including sexual activity within marriage and procreating children. These views follow logically from the Gnostic view that the body is part of the evil material world. However, even among early Christians, views against marriage and sex were common. They may trace back to Paul's affirming celibacy in light of his expectation that Jesus would return shortly (1 Cor. 7:8–9, 25–38). At any rate, many believers began to foreswear marriage and family and wealth in order to focus completely on God. To pagan culture, this was offensive and disruptive to the social order, especially when married persons quit having sex with their spouses in order to become wholly devoted to God. This social drama regularly recurs in these non-canonical documents. Take note that the Gnostic devaluation of the physical world and the human body also led to the opposite attitude toward sex. If the body is evil and does not matter, then some Gnostic adherents logically conclude that they can copulate with anyone, any time, in any form. Some scholars assert that early versions of this promiscuous mind-set are addressed by several NT writers (2 Pet. 2:10–22; 1 Jn 3:7–10, 4:1–3; 2 Jn 1:7; Jude 4–16). However, this opposite "anything goes" ethical posture is rare in these documents, which for the most part advocate denying sexuality even in marriage.

A third factor in these documents is false attribution. The names of Biblical personages attached to these genres— supposed "gospels," narrative "acts," and apostolic "epistles"—cannot possibly have been written by those people. This is because the documents are dated centuries later—almost unanimously by scholars of various persuasions. Hence, these documents often are called *"pseudepigrapha,"* literally meaning "false writing," because the writers named cannot be the actual authors.

The lineup below covers three categories of documents: those claiming to be *gospels*, those claiming to be *acts* or narratives of an apostle, and then two of those claiming to be *epistles* (there are many more). It does not go on to cover a fourth literature category, that of *apocalypse*—which is related, but somewhat outside the scope of our investigation. For our purposes, we stay focused on the resurrection of Jesus, not so much on the future resurrection of humans that is anticipated in the end times. For the following sources, each entry includes its estimated time of writing, its original language, its general content, and some of its historical problems or conflicts with NT narratives. Most of the following information on these non-canonical documents results from the commendable scholarship of David Brakke and Bart D. Ehrman.[36]

Documents That Claim Gospel Status

Infancy Gospel of James, also called Protoevangelium. In Greek. Second century AD, late. Very popular, more than a hundred Greek manuscripts survive, and more in many other languages.

---

[36] David Brakke, *The Apocryphal Jesus* (Chantilly, VA: The Teaching Company, 2017), and Bart D. Ehrman, *Lost Christianities: Christian Scriptures and the Battles over Authentication* (Chantilly, VA: The Teaching Company, 2002).

It focuses on the upbringing of Mary the mother of Jesus, why she is chosen to be the vessel of God's son, and how she remains a lifelong virgin. *Problems.* The stories of Mary's birth and childhood appear lifted straight out of the OT account of the prophet Samuel's boyhood; the book portrays Joseph as a widower with grown children, taking Mary as his second wife but disinterested in sleeping with her, due to his age.

Infancy Gospel of Thomas. In Greek or Syriac in the original. Coptic version found in 1945 in Nag Hammadi, Egypt. Second century AD, middle. It covers the years of Jesus's life from ages five to twelve. It affirms Jesus's power to transform things with just a word. *Problems.* The book portrays Jesus as a boy who curses and kills playmates for muddying his water pools or colliding with him; he also renders comatose a teacher who reprimands him; he makes up for this bullying behavior by healing or raising from the dead some accident victims; he also famously models birds out of clay and brings them to life, a story often depicted in medieval art.

Gospel of Peter. In Greek. Fragmentary. Second century AD, usually dated after the four gospels, as the unknown author shows signs of reading the gospel of Matthew, as well as the book of Revelation. It is found in 1886 in Akhmim, Egypt, buried in a coffin with a monk. It is mentioned as heresy by Serapion, Bishop of Antioch and by Origen (both circa third century AD); but it is never actually found until the discovery of these excerpts in Egypt by French archaeologists. The writing focuses on the trial of Jesus, a strange resurrection scene, and the resulting consternation of Pilate and the Jewish leaders. *Problems.* Jesus does not suffer on the cross (shades of the Docetic or Gnostic mindset); Herod Antipas orders Jesus's crucifixion while Pilate is exonerated, and the Jewish leaders excoriated; a skyscraping, gigantic Jesus figure leaves his tomb trailed by a walking, talking cross.

Egerton Gospel or Unknown Gospel. In Greek. Second century AD, middle. Sometimes called "Papyrus Egerton 2." It consists of a handful of small fragments from a codex or leaf book. It is found in Egypt, exact place unknown, because it is obtained in a collection bought by the British Museum through antiquities dealers in 1934. It captures a handful of recognizable instances in the life of Jesus that are reported in other sources. Jesus advises Jewish rulers to search the scriptures to see what Moses says about him (see Jn 5:39–46); he escapes death by stoning (see Jn 10:31–39); he cleanses a leper (see Mk 1:40–42); he is questioned about paying taxes (see Mk 12:14); and he stretches his hand over the Jordan River to make the water produce fruit, reminiscent of a fanciful scene involving sowing seed in a field that is featured in the Infancy Gospel of Thomas (see Mk 12:1–2). Some scholars imagine this document is an early-stage writing in the middle of the first century AD, written before the gospels of Mark and John. If true, this early date would allow it possibly to have served as a source for either or both gospel authors. *Problems.* Certain improvements on Mark's gospel in grammar or context that exist in the gospels of Matthew and Luke also arise in these fragments, a giveaway that these must be dated later; the document blends lines from different gospels, selecting and reconnecting phrases, signaling a later date and probable dependence on oral tradition derived from the gospel writings; there is no customary attestation or quotations from later church leaders, nor are there any other known papyri that would verify the distribution of this supposedly early gospel.[37]

Gospel of Truth. In Coptic. Dated to c. AD 130. Found in 1945, in Nag Hammadi, Egypt. It is attributed to Valentinus (c. AD 100–175), the codifier of Gnostic teaching whose works are lost except possibly for this one. Until this discovery, his works were known because of the ire he drew in diatribes from early Christian patristic fathers who quoted him. This work, a major Gnostic text, poetically captures a rapturous joy and gratitude to God for salvation from the body and from material things. *Problems.*

---

[37] Craig A. Evans, *Fabricating Jesus* (Downers Grove, IL: InterVarsity Press, 2006), 85–92. Also see Harry Y. Gamble, "Egerton Papyrus 2," in Freedman, ed., *Anchor Bible Dictionary*, vol. 2, 317–18.

The book claims that Jesus is killed by the rulers for delivering Gnostic truth; no mention is made of the resurrection of Jesus.

Gospel of Thomas. In Coptic, original probably in Greek. Second century AD, first half. Found in 1945, in Nag Hammadi, Egypt. Comprised of 114 sayings with no narratives. Complete text. It may in form resemble the document known as Q that many scholars believe was accessible to the authors of Matthew and Luke. Some sayings contain familiar NT images: the mustard seed, the speck in another's eye, the blind leading the blind. A major Gnostic text, it asserts that the sayings are secret and only those who interpret them correctly will reach eternal life. *Problems.* The book claims to be written by the twin brother of Jesus; it views women as inferior, but they too can be saved by knowledge if first they are transformed into men.

Gospel of Philip. In Coptic, original probably in Greek or Syriac. Second century AD, first half. Found in 1945, in Nag Hammadi, Egypt, in the same codex as the Gospel of Thomas. It bears the name of Philip because he is the only apostle mentioned by name, and because he held special status among Gnostics as the carrier of Jesus's revelation. The text compiles lists of statements and episodes including a few from the gospels (Matthew, John) without any narrative framework. One notorious passage suggests kissing between Mary Magdalene and Jesus, but the body part kissed is missing in the damaged text, and could be cheeks, hands, or feet, not necessarily lips. Even if mouth-kissing is in view, in the context the author's point is to elevate Mary to equal status with the disciples, to make her a source of special knowledge, not to assert a romantic relationship. *Problems:* The book presents a shape-shifting Jesus; it portrays an odd paint-stirring miracle of mixing 72 colors to produce a tub of white; it advocates advancing to higher levels in the Gnostic schematic, including a mysterious bridal chamber that unites the self with its original androgynous nature, in an act defined as resurrection in this life before one dies.[38]

---

[38] Wesley W. Isenberg, "Gospel of Philip," in Freedman, ed., *Anchor Bible Dictionary,* vol. 5, 312–13. Also, Craig A. Evans, *Fabricating Jesus,* 94, 211–12.

Gospel of Mary. In Coptic and in Greek fragments. Third century AD. Discovered in 1896 in a papyrus codex dated to the fifth century AD. When Jesus ascends, Mary Magdalene bucks up the disciples, telling them to be courageous and that God will protect them. Mary gives a secret teaching from Jesus about the soul ascending, causing dissension in the disciples. There is an undertone of contesting the limits of apostolic authority. *Problems.* Peter is portrayed as an unrepentant chauvinist; Jesus is shown saying that the world is not real, and that sin is only ignorance, both of which are views that border on Gnosticism.

Secret Gospel of Mark. In Greek. Dating disputed due to the high probability of forgery. Supposedly a first-century gospel is quoted in a second-century letter, then this letter is copied much later in the eighteenth century in a distinctive handwritten script typical of that era. This copy allegedly is found in 1958 in a monastery near Jerusalem, in a book of collected letters by Ignatius of Antioch (d. 108). The document is hidden, not available today. Ostensibly it is a letter from Clement of Alexandria (c. 180) to an unknown Theodore, asserting there is a secret version of the gospel of Mark. The letter excerpts several accounts from this supposed gospel. In one, the Jesus figure refuses to see a few women disciples, and in another he is unclothed as he baptizes a young man at night. *Problems.* The document cannot be examined currently; the baptism story carries homosexual overtones; no other historical evidence points to the existence of a second and secret gospel by Mark; the now deceased professor who found the letter is virtually certain to have been the perpetrator of this hoax.[39]

Gospel of Judas. In Coptic. Second Century AD, middle. Found near Al-Minya, Egypt in the late 1970s by unnamed treasure hunters, but publishing was prevented until 2006. The finding

---

[39] An expert in detecting forgeries obtained a photograph of the Clementine letter. He conclusively determined that the handwriting style periodically veers into the professor's own idiosyncratic Greek mode, as uncovered in his papers and marginal notes. See Craig A. Evans, *Fabricating Jesus,* 94–97, 260.

confirmed a mention by Irenaeus (d. 202) of a book with this title that he dismissed as a work of the Gnostics. The book consists of dialogs between Jesus and his disciples, including Judas, with virtually no narratives. The disciples come in for harsh criticism from the Jesus figure (Judas less so) because they worship the lower, wrong deity. When Jesus challenges the disciples to tell him his true identity, Judas mouths the Gnostic slant that he is a messenger of knowledge (not savior from sin) from the remote true deity. Judas alone receives special revelation from Jesus. The Jesus figure departs in his divine nature, leaving behind his human body, which Judas duly betrays. Judas is rewarded by becoming the ruler of all of those of Adam's race who save themselves and join the divine spirits through knowledge. *Problems.* The book gives little historical data, but rather a detailed description of standard Gnostic beliefs and myths about spiritual dimensions; its revisionism of Judas's role conflicts with other, historically grounded accounts; the key dialog with Judas appears to be modeled on the gospel accounts of Peter identifying Jesus as the Messiah who is sent by the one true God.

Documents That Claim to Narrate Acts of the Apostles

Acts of John. In Greek, Latin. Second century AD, second half. Probably because John gets so few scenes in the canonical NT book of Acts by Luke, this book aims to balance it by giving wider coverage to John's actions. It also may be intending in part to correct extreme views against sexuality. It holds that the danger lies in the heart and the will, not in the body and its impulses. *Problems.* Jesus is portrayed not as human, but only as divine, frequently shape-shifting; his body does not have to undergo suffering, incorporating the typical Gnostic overtones; John is credited with initially bringing the gospel to Ephesus, in contrast to the NT which says Paul brings it; John orders obedient bedbugs to amass at the door while the disciples slumber at an inn; a farmer sleeps with a married woman, then in shame cuts off his private parts with a scythe and flings them at the house of his lover, then repents of his self-mutilation and follows John.

Acts of Peter. In Greek, Coptic, Latin. Second century AD, second half. Fragmentary, to the point that some scholars dispute whether there was ever a full-length work that included all the fragments. The Coptic version is found in 1945 in Nag Hammadi, Egypt. Other versions include two main accounts. The first one depicts a duel of miracles between the magician Simon Magus and Peter, who triumphs with God's greater power. The second one presents Peter being crucified head down, but not dying until he waxes eloquent about the way the world has been upside down since Adam, and only repentance can straighten things out. The Coptic version features a painful drama. Peter's beautiful daughter is kidnapped as a pre-teen by a rich old man who wants to marry her, over the objections of Peter's wife. In an act of divine interference, the girl is paralyzed in half of her body, an affliction she previously faced intermittently. The unsuitable suitor returns her to Peter's home. At one point, Peter heals her, then reverses it and re-afflicts her with paralysis, to protect her from any other lustful suitors. The rich man repents, dies, and wills a field to Peter. He sells it, and gives the proceeds to the poor. *Problems.* Peter's daughter is manipulated by both her suitor and her father, instead of being healed; Peter displays the standard obsession with suppressing even marital sexuality, for his daughter could regain her health and marry a worthy man; also, in some versions, his preaching persuades women to leave their pagan husbands, who then plot to kill him; no other records from reliable sources corroborate these lamentable attitudes in Peter.

Acts of Paul (and Thecla). In Greek. Second century AD, late. Fragmentary. This adventure story was very popular. Paul is seen converting multiple Greek and Roman households, transforming their greed to generosity to the poor. Later, he also converts soldiers guarding the emperor. A young aristocratic woman in Iconium named Thecla hears Paul preach and breaks off her engagement. She forms a chaste crush on Paul, follows him, endures trials, makes daring escapes, then emerges as a prominent though cave-dwelling faith teacher. *Problems.* When Nero orders Paul beheaded, milk not blood spouts forth from his body, alluding apparently to the metaphor that the gospel is milk to the new convert; Paul is depicted giving a special blessing to men who do not sleep with their wives—affirming a message that eternal life comes to those who abstain from sexual relations, even within marriage (in contrast to 1 Tim. 4:1–5).

Acts of Thomas. Original in Syriac, translated to Greek. Third century AD, first half. Complete text. Follows Thomas on his mission to India. What the Gospel of Thomas recommends, the Acts of Thomas dramatizes incessantly: people giving up sex and the accumulation of wealth to devote themselves wholly to Jesus. In prison, Thomas sings *"The Hymn of the Pearl,"* a parable of a prince as a soul who leaves the world's impurity and finds the pearl of salvation, which is the knowledge that the real world is spiritual not material. *Problems.* The work claims Thomas is the brother of Jesus; no resurrection of the body is foreseen as it must be left behind, so that only the soul lives on; a Jesus figure appears in a bridal chamber in India to convince the new couple not to consummate, not to have children in order to avoid the distractions they cause, but instead to marry their individual souls to God.

Acts of Andrew. In Greek, Coptic. Third century AD. Fragmentary. Two main accounts survive. In the first, a city of cannibals tortures Andrew. He is saved by an intervention of Jesus. Revived, Andrew floods the city until it repents. The other account takes place in Achaia, Greece. Andrew's preaching inspires a married woman to give up sex with her husband, who happens to be a proconsul. Despite protests, the proconsul crucifies Andrew. *Problems.* No city of cannnibals in this part of the world is documented in other sources; flooding a town is not really a fair strategy for evangelism; the social context of the time may mean the story is less about liberating women and more about a power competition between pagan and Christian societies.

Documents That Claim to Be Epistles from the Apostles

The Epistle of Barnabas. In Greek. Dated to AD 130–135. Found in 1844 on Mount Sinai, Egypt at St. Catherine's Monastery, within a collection that included all NT books (called Codex Sinaiticus, c. 325). Originally anonymous, the book later is attributed falsely to Barnabas, a fellow missionary with Paul. The book contends the laws of Moses were symbolic not literal, e.g., circumcision symbolizes the crucifixion of Jesus. Because the Israelites broke covenant with God in the OT, and the Jewish leaders rejected God's Son in the NT, God has rejected the entire people. He has replaced them with Christians, and the OT promises apply only to Christians, not to the Jews. *Problems.* Venomous tone against the Jews leads to the view that they are enemies of God and must be punished or eliminated (in contrast to Rom. 11:1–15). This letter almost made it into the NT canon. Providentially, it did not. It was deservedly scuttled to the ash heap of pseudepigraphical history.

3 Corinthians. In Greek. Second century AD, second half. Included in some versions with the *Acts of Paul*. As if in an email chain, the letter starts with a letter from the Corinthians, which Paul, the falsely claimed author, purportedly then answers. It is easy to see the author's motivation. The Corinthian letter says two false teachers are leading people astray with typical teachings of Gnosticism. They say that the OT is useless, because it depicts a lower deity who trapped divine spirits in material bodies. Jesus does not have a real body, does not suffer when he dies, but brings the knowledge that liberates elite souls from their bodies, with no future resurrection necessary. In contrast, the author insistently asserts that because Jesus was raised physically, Christians who believe in him also will be raised physically in bodily form. *Problems.* It is for a good, orthodox cause that the writing corrects false teaching, yet the author falsely impersonates Paul; the author misses the nuance from Paul that the resurrection body will be a physical body but will be "spiritual" and "changed" in some way (1 Cor. 15:44, 50–53; see chapter 2 and addition 4).

Sorting Out Sources is Essential for Historical Investigation

These falsely attributed documents contain little of historical value other than to reflect what people of that era may have thought and imagined. We cannot use them to determine what in history actually may have happened to Jesus or to his witnesses. The entertainment value is there however, copiously evident in these short descriptions. Perhaps that value of entertainment itself was uppermost in the motives of some of the authors while others clearly wanted to correct what they perceived to be wrongheaded beliefs. Yet none of these documents measure up to our criteria of historicity. That is why they are not used in this historical investigation of the resurrection. (Note: to review the historical criteria and how the resurrection narrative measures up on the strength of its legitimate sources, see addition 3 in the main book.)

This resource on documents has introduced the authors and overall content for the major first-century writings that are drawn upon in the main book for the lines of evidence for the resurrection of Jesus. This resource also helps you see why other documents in circulation during the two centuries after Jesus's time do not deserve to be part of our investigation. For the key writings that make the cut to be in our selected sources, the next resource shows how the general dates for the original composition of the documents are estimated.

RESOURCE

ESTIMATING DOCUMENT DATES

istorians get a little jittery when they have to struggle to date their sources. Today, this is rarely a problem. Nearly every book or article published, in print or online, includes a clear date of writing or publishing. In the ancient Near East, this was not the case. Few authors would put dates on their writings, and some did not bother to give themselves a byline, making their writings anonymous. The exception is when people wrote letters. Then usually it was clear from whom the letter came, and often though not always, to whom it was sent. This practice helps in the NT where after the first five books (the four gospels and Acts) the rest of the books are letters, with the possible exceptions of Hebrews and Revelation. Even in the letter genre, dates usually were not included.

As a result, dating ancient works becomes a form of scholarly sport, and subject to debate. Getting dates reasonably precise can add to or detract from the credibility of the document. It can determine whether authors were eyewitnesses or could interview eyewitnesses to an event, or whether they are writing well after the event, in effect writing as historians based on their research.

Factors That Affect Date Estimates

What factors enter into the document dating debates? Most factors are obvious, others not so much.

- Events and names the author mentions clearly exist before the work is written.
- Events and names known to exist around the authors' eras that they nevertheless omit, may show that the writing takes place before these occur.
- If other later authors refer to their writing, then these documents are written and distributed before the later authors, establishing a "no later than" boundary for the dates.
- When a document we are trying to date quotes another author whose dates we know, this provides a "no earlier than" boundary.
- Language style, terminology for official positions, or descriptions of buildings can help with dating when these factors are known through other forms of research, such as linguistic studies, or archaeological excavations (see the Found in the Ground Index).
- When an early manuscript copy of a document is discovered, whether it is partial or complete, the data existing at the site where it is found (coins, pottery and more) can help date the copy and then add input for dating the original manuscript.
- Other content elements in the document itself can help build a sequence of events that can influence dating schemes.

These factors, then, are among the ways scholars date documents. We can apply them as needed to our brief look at the two main alternative dating grids for the gospels and the book of Acts.

The Best Place to Start the Dating of the Gospels

One of the best places to start in dating the gospels is not with any of the four gospels but with Acts, the sequel Luke writes to his gospel. The reason for this is a matter of logic, with certain assumptions. Luke himself states that he wrote Acts after he wrote his gospel; he writes them both to the same patron (Lk 1:3–4; Acts 1:1). Therefore, the gospel precedes Acts. Then the gospel of Luke clearly uses another gospel, the gospel of Mark, as one of its sources, adopting nearly half of Mark's material. So Mark must be written before Luke and Acts are written. This historical sequence drives most gospel dating grids (though a minority of scholars hold that Matthew precedes Mark).

The book of Acts ends its narrative abruptly with Paul under house arrest in Rome. The tone however is almost celebratory. Paul can receive any visitors he wishes and can teach freely, right in the heart of the world capital of Rome. The date for Paul's residence in Rome is not specified in Acts. It is determined by taking the anchor date of AD 51–52 when Paul stays in Corinth (see chapter 7) on his second major journey, then calculating the time elapsed along the way between his major extended stopovers in Ephesus (AD 54–56) and Caesarea (AD 57–59). It is about AD 60 when Paul arrives at Rome. The reigning emperor is Nero. Nero begins a historically verified persecution of Christians about AD 64, continuing to the end of his reign in AD 68. Later Christian writers assert that both Peter (c. AD 64) and Paul (c. AD 67) perish in the Neronic persecution.

For our investigation, we have to ask the following question: Why does Luke not mention the denouement of his two main protagonists in Acts? Scholars give various answers.

- Because Luke wrote *before* either one of them dies.
- Because Luke was *embarrassed* to record the deaths of these martyrs, afraid it would hurt the evangelistic outreach.
- Because Luke himself *dies* in the early AD 60s after writing Acts.

- Because Luke's *literary intent* was to show how the apostles take the gospel outward until they fulfill their mission, which they complete by reaching the world capital of Rome.

Now a second, equally striking question arises. Why does Luke not mention the destruction of Jerusalem by the Romans in AD 70?

According to Josephus, more than a million Jews die in the siege and eventual massacre (*War* 6.9.3). Some scholars discredit that huge death toll, but Josephus asserts it resulted from the timing of the capture, when the Feast of Unleavened Bread (including Passover) swelled the population of Jerusalem. In any event, the destruction was devastating. It rocked the Jewish world, ended the priesthood, and started the rabbinic tradition of preserving Jewish faith through the synagogue and Torah, no longer through the demolished temple and its sacrificial system. Why is there no mention in Acts of this event if Luke writes after it happens? Again, scholars offer different answers.

- Because Luke wrote *before* the temple was destroyed.
- Because Luke was *extra clever.* He leaves Jesus's prophecy of temple destruction dangling out there in his gospel, and neither there nor in Acts does he state its fulfillment. Yet everyone who would read his gospel would know what had happened. This way it seems more like Jesus really said and predicted it, when in reality Luke just *retrojected* it—putting invented words in Jesus's mouth after the fact (Lk 21:5-6).
- Because Luke, like the other gospel writers, was theologically focused and not to be bothered about the *historical detail* of the temple being toppled and burned to the ground.

It should be noted here that the primary reason scholars often date the gospels and Acts late is the way they interpret the passages in the gospels where Jesus predicts the temple destruction (Mk 13:14; Mt 22:7, 24:15; Lk 19:43–44, 21:20–24). They assume because the temple was in fact destroyed forty years later, the predictions must have been retrojected. This comes from a hidden assumption that no one can ever predict the future. Yet it is not too hard to imagine that Jesus could prophesy the destruction of the temple with some accurate details, when it had suffered a similar fate slightly more than 600 years earlier. That perilous moment involved an army surrounding it, building siege works, and burning down the temple (compare 2 Kings 25:1, 8–10 with Lk 19:43–44, 21:20). Other scholars interpret Jesus's prediction of temple destruction in the gospels as applying to the end times, shortly before his anticipated return to earth. In this case, the predictions pose no issue for the estimated dates for the writing of the gospels. One can see how pre-ordained perspectives often enter into supposedly objective scholarly dating of biblical documents.[40]

Two Major Dating Schemes, Earlier and Later

For now, we can distill the gospel dating schemes down to two major alternatives. They divide primarily over the issue of whether the writers produce their gospels before or after the temple is destroyed in AD 70. The two views diverge over their explanations for why the temple destruction is not mentioned — neither in Acts nor in any of the gospels.

The earlier-date grid takes the straightforward position that the account of the demolished temple is omitted because it had not yet happened when the writers wrote. Therefore, Acts would be written by the early or mid-AD 60s, Luke earlier in the 60s or later 50s (some schemes seem to like the range AD 59–63) and Mark at the latest in the late 50s.

The later-date grid assumes the view that the destroyed temple was not referenced by Luke in Acts due to literary purposes, or

---

[40] Brant Pitre, *The Case for Jesus* (New York, NY: Image, 2016), 90-94.

due to keeping the focus theological not political—so as not to alienate either the Romans or Jewish people. This grid usually positions Acts in the upper AD 80s, the gospel of Luke in the lower 80s and Mark in the 70s. This sequence does not directly determine where Matthew and John are dated; but it does put the interpolated source of the "Q" collection in the mix, as a predecessor or contemporary of Mark (who does not use it) but prior to Luke and Matthew (who do use it). Also relevant are the dates for the letters of Paul. It is generally agreed that all would have been written throughout the decade of the AD 50s, give or take a year or two on either side (see chapter 7). The two dating grids form the chart below.

TWO DOCUMENT DATING ESTIMATES
ALL YEARS AD

Document	Earlier Grid	Later Grid
"Q" source (probable)	40s-50s	40s-70s
Paul's letters	50s-early 60s	50s-early 60s
Mark	50s-60s	70s
Luke	60s	80s
Acts	60s	80s
Matthew	60s	70s-80s
John	60s-90s	90s

Some may wonder whether Mark can be dated even earlier. It is possible, though not probable. Because Mark has a falling out with Paul on the first missionary journey (in the first year probably, though the mission runs about AD 47–48), it would take Mark some elapsed time to be rehabilitated (Acts 15:37–40). According to both later Christian writers and NT data, Mark was close to Peter. Peter likely helped him recover, just as Jesus had helped Peter overcome his disastrous denials in the hour of testing. Paul indicates he reconciles with Mark in a letter probably written from a prison in Rome, about AD 60 (Col. 4:10). The late AD 40s and early 50s were probably Mark's time to mature and recover his reputation, so he probably could not have written or distributed his gospel before the mid-50s. Few would assert a date before then. The fact that Paul knows Mark but does not mention his gospel in later letters may mean Mark writes it in the late 50s or early 60s, still in time for a chain reaction of the writings of Matthew, Luke and Acts, before the Jerusalem cataclysm of AD 70.

Other Strangely Omitted Yet Significant Events

Several other verified events come into play to favor the early dates. The destruction of Jerusalem is *completed* in AD 70, but the resilience of the Jewish defenders enables them to hold off the Romans for four years prior to their ultimate defeat. This elapsed time means that the Romans start their siege of Jerusalem in AD 66. Of the five works (the gospels and Acts) that the later grid dates after AD 70, none of them mention the *beginning* of the siege either.

Taking this one step further, another major event for the early church occurs in AD 62. James, the brother of Jesus and the leader of the "mother church" in Jerusalem, suffers a "judicial" murder by the high priest. This priest is a descendant of Annas, the power-broker priest behind the scenes in the arrest and trial of Jesus. This travesty is recorded by Josephus (*Antiquities* 20.9.1). James is martyred while Paul remains in Rome. Again, there is no mention of the death of James in Acts. It seems odd for Luke not to mention the fate of James when Luke puts him center stage at a crucial juncture at the council in Acts 15. Plus, the Jerusalem church with James as its leader continually receives mention in Acts as a lodestone for Paul when he travels through the city on his journeys (Acts 15:2, 18:22, 21:15–17).

Favoring the earlier grid are these five non-mentions of major events: the death of James in Jerusalem, the deaths of Peter and Paul in a brutal persecution wave in Rome, the four-year siege of Jerusalem, and the final destruction of the temple. These non-mentions not only occur in Acts, which presents itself as a history of evangelism by the early church; these non-mentions also occur in all of the gospels. One would expect maybe one or more major event would sneak by this guild of silence and attract mention from even one author—that is, unless the original manuscripts were written *before* any of these events happened.

At any rate, these major documents for the resurrection all are bracketed within the first century, by either dating grid. The earlier dates allow for more plentiful eyewitness contact by the authors, but the later dates do not eliminate the possibility. A person 25-30 years old in AD 30 might still be alive fifty years later in the AD 80s. Moreover, the authors likely would collect material from firsthand or secondhand witnesses years before they sat down to write. The nature of oral transmission of data in Jewish culture could preserve many of the sayings as well as the deeds of Jesus over a twenty to thirty-year period in the earlier grid, or even a fifty-year period in the later grid (see resource 1).

Other Time Gaps in Biographical Literature

To put things in context, we can compare other elapsed times in first-century authorship. By this we mean the time gaps between the point when ancient authors wrote down records, and the earlier point when the various events actually occurred. (Note that author lifespans are indicated next to their names.)

Josephus (AD 37–100) writes 5–1500 years later than recorded events.
Tacitus (AD 56–100) writes 30–100 years later.
Suetonius (AD 69–130) writes 25–170 years later.
Plutarch (AD 50–120) writes 30–600 years later.

For the events of the crucifixion and resurrection occurring in the same year within the range of AD 30–33, the gospel authors write between 25–65 years later at the most, and Paul just 20–30 years later (see resource 3).

One related factor to note carries its own significance. When we take (1) the number of manuscript copies for the NT documents in their *original* languages, (2) the *earliest* copy extant, (3) the estimated *time elapsed* between original and copy, and then compare them to the works of major Greco-Roman authors, there would be no contest. The NT wins these other measures of historical reliability hands down.[41]

Compared to the major political and military figures in the Greek and Roman worlds covered by other ancient authors, the supposedly obscure prophet Jesus of Nazareth does not wait long for his biographies. What is more, as we saw elsewhere in the main book (chapter 7), the *preaching* of the resurrection finds strong historical support for being dated significantly earlier than the *writing* of the gospels. That is the case for whichever grid we use, the earlier one or the later one. The preaching of the resurrection is dated within about five years of the event, based on Paul's written evidence in 1 Corinthians, and within fifty days, based on Luke's record in Acts. The resurrection narrative predates the gospel writings by several decades. It stands on its own no matter where in these ranges one is inclined to date the gospel books themselves.

---

[41] Matt Slick, "Manuscript Evidence for Superior New Testament Reliability,"carm.org, *Christian Apologetics and Research Ministry*, 10 Dec 2008. It contains useful charts on secular sources and on NT document fragments. For another good chart directly comparing secular sources and specific biblical sources, along with contextual comments, see also Jimmy Williams, "Are the Biblical Documents Reliable?" probe.org, *Probe Ministries*, 27 May 2015.

RESOURCE

3

RESOURCE 3

CALCULATING TIMELINES FOR RESURRECTION WEEK AND YEAR

No document in either the New Testament or in our known secular sources denotes a specific date, day of the week, or year when Jesus dies on the cross. For centuries, scholars have sought to determine this date based on correlating available sets of data. In our era we have more data than ever before, due especially to computer software applied to ancient calendars and astronomical systems.

The range of data sets used to establish dates includes the following sources.

- The NT documents, the gospels and especially Luke, along with certain letters from Paul.
- Texts from the first-century Greco-Roman culture.
- The years of the reigns of Roman emperors, according to their records.
- Calendars of the Jews, Romans and other ancient Near Eastern cultures.
- Systematic astronomical data, going forward or backward in time, easier to access than ever before through software programs.

Before we proceed any further, I must note that this type of excursion into specific timeline schemes is *not important for faith* in relation to the events of the cross and the resurrection. In the main book, I have offered nine lines of evidence that raise the historical probability of the resurrection. Only one line of evidence deals with specific dates (see main book, chapter 7). Even that line of evidence does not depend on determining or agreeing on an exact date for the "passion" week of Jesus, which I also will term "resurrection" week. The NT writings are concerned with events and witnesses and the meaning of these events— the main events being the crucifixion, the resurrection, and the giving of the Spirit. But the NT authors do not date these events precisely. That lack of dating is not an uncommon factor in other first-century writings. Still, with so much evidence available, it is worth looking at whether dates can be estimated, out of curiosity if nothing else. The effort can produce several alternative scenarios. Having alternatives may help some gospel readers who wrestle with certain apparent discrepancies in the timelines of the gospel narratives. Because of the data sets involved, subject to scientific and historical interpretation, conclusions on the dates for resurrection week remain to a certain degree tentative.

Where to begin? Usually we would assume the place to begin is with the year when Jesus is born. Ironically, the year of his birth has less reliable data than the year when he dies on the cross. For the record, most scholars date the birth of Jesus in the range 4–6 BC, based on the well-documented date for the death of the ruler of Israel at the time, Herod the Great, in 4 BC.[42]

Pilate, Tiberius and John the Baptist Assist with Estimates

For us, a better place to begin is with some well-established historical facts about Jesus as an adult. One of the most accepted facts is that Jesus is executed under the prefecture of Pontius Pilate. From the secular Jewish-Roman historian Josephus (*Antiquities*

---

[42] "Chronology of Jesus,"wikipedia.org, retrieved 2 April 2017.

18.3.1, 18.4.2), we know that Pilate's term in office as prefect of Judea lasts ten years, from AD 26–36. That sets up a ten-year range (or eleven-year range with months on either end) for the year when Jesus is crucified. Here usually we will refer to the cross event as the date we are seeking, with the understanding for believers that the resurrection event is included in that same week.

A second highly attested historical fact about Jesus is that his public career emerges *after* the ministry of his relative, John the Baptist (Lk 1:36, 3:15–22). The figure of John the Baptist is mentioned not only by all four gospel writers, but also by Josephus (*Antiquities* 18.5.2). Luke's account of John the Baptist coming on the scene offers a rich set of data by which to correlate dates.

> *In the fifteenth year of Tiberius Caesar—when Pontius Pilate was governor of Judea, Herod tetrarch of Galilee, his brother Philip tetrarch of Iturea and Traconitis, and Lysanias tetrarch of Abilene—during the high-priesthood of Annas and Caiaphas, the word of God came to John son of Zechariah in the wilderness. (Luke 3:1–2)*

All of these leaders are documented in secular sources, but the key date for our purposes is the *"fifteenth year of Tiberius Caesar."* To calculate the fifteenth year, we need to know which year was the first year of Tiberius. From Roman records, we know the famed emperor Augustus (formerly known as Octavian) precedes Tiberius. Augustus dies in August, AD 14. So we start the clock on the reign of Tiberius in September, AD 14. (There is some dispute on whether the clock should start sooner due to Tiberius being appointed a co-emperor in the last two years of Augustus; however these years are not counted by the Roman historians Tacitus and Suetonius, so we will not count them either). The first year of Tiberius then runs from September, AD 14 to the end of August, AD 15. Counting through the second through the fifteenth year brings that year to the timespan of September, AD 28 to August, AD 29. By this logic, within that yearlong span, John the Baptist begins his ministry. We do not know how long the ministry of the Baptist continues.

We do know that Jesus is baptized by John the Baptist, which is a truly startling factor in that cultural context, and therefore historically highly probable. That is because of the way it pictures Jesus in a subservient position, as if he needs cleansing, when he is the savior in the story. It is not exactly what one would expect from writers claiming that Jesus is the Messiah. Yet we do not know when precisely Jesus is baptized. From the rapid rhythm in the accounts of John the Baptist, it is reasonable to conjecture that this baptism takes place in the first year of John's ministry, although not necessarily within the first four months. So the earliest year for the baptism and beginning of Jesus's own ministry is AD 29, except in the unlikely event that he starts almost concurrently with John in the autumn of AD 28. After his baptism, Jesus begins his own career in ministry in Galilee, and John continues in parallel, until he is imprisoned.

Returning to our range of years based on the term of Pilate, we eliminate three years, AD 26, 27 and 28 from the list of years when Jesus could undergo the cross.

Another historically strong fact regarding Jesus's death on the cross is that it occurs in the springtime. Passover week always occurs in the spring, usually in April or very late March. If Jesus were to be executed as early as the spring of AD 29, assuming John the Baptist does not begin his ministry until September AD 28, Jesus would not have time for even a full year of ministry—only about seven months—even if he joins the Baptist at the very outset. This does not fit with the gospel narratives, especially the gospel of John, where Jesus is recorded attending more than one Passover week in Jerusalem. Therefore, we eliminate as well the year AD 29 for the crucifixion.

Knowing the exact length of the ministry of Jesus would be useful at this point, but the gospels are not completely clear on this timespan. Scholars agree that the ministry lasts between one and three-and-a-half years, but within that range there are disputes. John's gospel seems to cover at least three if not four Passover festivals (Jn 2:13, 6:4, 11:55, a fourth possibly though not probably in Jn 5:1). A set of three Passovers entails at least a two-year ministry, with four entailing at least a three-year ministry. The other three gospels are not specific about Passovers, except for the week when Jesus is crucified.

If Jesus joins John the Baptist in late AD 28, or early in the first three months of AD 29, then that allows time for a year of ministry, before potentially being executed as soon as April of AD 30. The first three gospels allow for this time frame, though the gospel of John would not.

If we extend that logic, then a two-year ministry ends with Jesus on the cross in April, AD 31, which John's time frame can permit. If the span of ministry for Jesus is three years, then that would put the cross in April, AD 32. Can we push the ministry beyond three years to include AD 33 for the cross? If Jesus joins up with John the Baptist late in AD 29, say within the last two months, then if the crucifixion takes place in April, AD 33, his ministry lasts about three-and-a-half years. It is a tight squeeze to be sure, however this appears to qualify as the last year the crucifixion could happen, given our assumptions. From this logic we can eliminate the rest of the years of Pilate's tenure, namely AD 34, 35 and 36.

These considerations narrow the possible years from eleven (AD 26–36) down to four, the years AD 30, 31, 32, and 33.

Precision in Passover Timing in the Jewish Calendar

At this juncture, our data from NT and secular texts runs dry in regard to distinguishing between these years. Fortunately, at this point, calendar and astronomical data come into play. Jewish calendar dates are different than those on our calendar, which is derived largely from the Roman calendar. Jewish calendars are lunar, based on the movements of the moon, while the Roman and most western calendars are solar, based on the sun. Nevertheless these can be connected.

From the OT, we know that the Jewish Passover day must occur on a specific date in a specific month. Like our individual birthdays, the day of the week changes but the date in the month never changes year to year. According to the OT, Passover begins at twilight, or sunset on the 14th day of the month of Aviv (Deut. 16:1; Lev. 23:5; Num. 28:16). Aviv, the first month in the Jewish year, is later commonly known as Nisan, after the Babylonian nomenclature that the Jewish calendar-keepers picked up during their captivity. The month of Aviv or Nisan corresponds approximately with our period of late March to April.

The Jewish 24-hour day *begins with evening*. It starts at sunset, then continues until sundown the next day (unlike the western day, that begins and ends at midnight). If the Passover begins at twilight on the 14th of Nisan, then that means the 14th of Nisan is ending, and the 15th of Nisan is beginning. This is because the Jewish day begins and ends at sunset. As a result, the Passover day is actually on the 15th of Nisan, starting in the evening and continuing to evening the next day, while the 14th of Nisan is the day before Passover.

Three of the gospels, based on Mark's original version, report that Jesus eats a Passover meal with his disciples the night before his crucifixion. Because Jesus dies on the day of preparation, the official Passover meal would occur that evening right after his body was laid in the tomb (this would be the case for any of the timelines we are considering). That creates a discrepancy between gospels on whether the Last Supper was the official Passover meal. Various explanations have been attempted. Perhaps Jesus scheduled the Passover meal a day early, or maybe it was not an official Passover-style meal (as the gospel of John implies, John 13:1–5, 23–28).[43] Another explanation suggests that the Galileans might have followed a different calendar than the Judeans, so that Galileans always would eat Passover earlier. At any rate, the common denominator remains that the disciples ate a meal with Jesus before he was arrested, put to trial and executed. At the meal, he explained to them the meaning of his impending death, before they headed out to the Garden of Gethsemane for the treacherous night (see chapter 9 in the main book).

---

[43] Jonathan Klawans, "Was Jesus' Last Supper a Seder?" Bible Review, Oct 2001, republished at biblicalarchaeology.org, Bible History Daily, *Biblical Archaeology Society*, Oct 2012.

The Day of Preparation Requires Definition

All four gospels indicate that Jesus dies on the cross on a day known as *"the day of Preparation"* (Mt 27:62, Mk 15:42, Lk 23:54, Jn 19:14, 31). The key question we run into is this: For which day is the day of preparation preparing?

The common understanding of the day of preparation is that it is the day before the Sabbath, the regular weekly Sabbath. For the Jews, the weekly Sabbath occurs on the last day of the week, the seventh day, which is our modern Saturday. Because Jewish days start the evening before, the Jewish Sabbath runs Friday evening at sunset to Saturday evening at sunset. This means the day of preparation for the weekly Sabbath is the day before, namely Thursday sunset to Friday sunset. Here let us pause to point out that we have happened upon the reason why most traditions place the death of Jesus on a Friday, traditionally called "Good Friday." That reckoning is based on the gospels asserting that Jesus dies on the day of preparation. The gospels never say he dies on the sixth day of the week. The gospel term *"day of Preparation"* is assumed to refer to the day, our Friday, that prepares for the regular weekly Sabbath, our Saturday.

This logic has led to the traditional timeline that Jesus dies on Friday afternoon, remains in the tomb Friday night and all day Saturday, then rises early Sunday morning, before the women encounter the empty tomb.

Based on this assumption of a Friday crucifixion, scholars have looked at our range of four years and asked whether any of the years have the Passover, the 15th of Nisan, occurring on a Saturday. That derives from the day of preparation, the 14th of Nisan, occuring on a Friday.

In fact, astronomical clocks wound backwards with reference to the Jewish calendar show that two of the four years have Nisan 14 occurring on a Friday. In AD 30, it occurs on our April 7. In AD 33, it occurs on our April 3 (though sometimes this is disputed as occurring not on Friday but on Saturday, April 4, which would disqualify AD 33 according to the formula we are using). These then appear to be our two choices for the date of Jesus dying on the cross, with the difference being whether the ministry of Jesus is about one year or as long as three-and-a-half years.[44]

The Traditional View Is the "Weekend-Stay" in the Tomb

These two dates satisfy most scholars and continue the traditional timeline of what we can call the "weekend stay." The journey from the cross to the tomb to the resurrection is completed in the time frame from Friday afternoon to Sunday morning.

For some gospel readers, this weekend timeline runs into the question of how many hours Jesus spends in the tomb. In this timeline, his body lays in the tomb Friday night (about six hours), all day and night Saturday (24 hours), and then at most five hours on Sunday morning (since the women find the tomb empty before dawn), for a total of 35 hours. Scholars assert that in the Jewish mind-set a *part* of a day counts as a *full* day. Under this assumption, Jesus rises on the third day, Sunday, even though he is only in the tomb for one full day, plus parts of two others, with a stay in the tomb of just two nights.

A discrepancy emerges when we hark back to the discussion on the sign of Jonah (see main book, chapters 3 and 9). Under public pressure to perform a sign, Jesus emphasizes that the sign of Jonah will be the only sign they will get from him. He applies the sign of Jonah to himself in two gospels, Matthew and Luke (Mt 12:38–41, 16:4, Lk 11:29–32). In Matthew, where he mentions it twice, he elaborates on and specifies the dimensions for that sign.

---

[44] "Crucifixion Passover Date" Passover dates 26-34 AD (sic), judaism vschristianity.com. http://www.usno.navy.mil/USNO/astronomical-applications/data-services/spring-phenom. (Please note that this site shows the day of preparation dates, Nisan 14, but labels them as 'Passover'; these dates are not actually Passover, which is Nisan 15. However, to the western mind, the Passover is celebrated the night of Nisan 14. The confusion rests in the fact that the new Jewish day begins at sunset.)

> *"For as Jonah was three days and three nights in the belly*
> *of a huge fish, so the Son of Man will be three days and*
> *three nights in the heart of the earth." (Matthew 12:40)*

Here it seems Jesus is claiming in no uncertain terms that he will be in the tomb for 72 hours, three days and three nights. Usually, by Jewish reckoning, a night was twelve hours and a day was twelve hours. As we noted, a night runs from sunset to sunrise, and a day runs from sunrise to sunset. Jesus seems to assume this definition of a day. At one point, the gospel of John quotes Jesus defining a day in just this way.

> *Jesus answered, "Are there not twelve hours of daylight?*
> *Anyone who walks in the daytime will not stumble, for*
> *they see by this world's light. It is when a person walks*
> *at night that they stumble, for they have no light."*
> *(John 11:9–10)*

The weekend-stay timeline does not allow for a full 72-hour duration in the tomb as Jesus apparently predicts for himself.

Is there any alternative scenario that might allow for the full 72 hours?

Note the Hidden Assumption in the Weekend-Stay Scenario

Now let's see. If we look back at how we arrived at the weekend-stay timeline, we can detect a hidden assumption. The weekend timeline takes the gospels' assertion that Jesus dies on the day of preparation. That is assumed to be Friday, before the Saturday Sabbath. Then this timeline looks for a Friday that matches up with the 14th of Nisan, to find a year within our range for the crucifixion. The hidden assumption is that the 14th of Nisan *must* occur on a Friday.

Friday is the day of preparation for the regular weekly Sabbath on Saturday. However, the weekend-stay timeline conflates the weekly Sabbath with the Passover. It *assumes* that the Passover occurs on Saturday the year that Jesus dies on the cross. If the Passover occurs on Saturday, then the day of preparation for the regular Sabbath is the same as the day of preparation for the Passover, both happening on the same Friday. Stop right there for a moment. Consider that it may not have happened that way. The gospels never say that Jesus dies on the sixth day of the week, which would *require* a Friday crucifixion. They say he dies on the day of preparation, which can *float* on different days of the week when it is the day of preparation for a floating holiday like the Passover.

The Passover can occur on any day of the week, but must occur on a specific date on the Jewish calendar, the 15th of Nisan. It could occur on a Saturday, but also on any other day. In most years it would not occur on a Saturday.

There Can Be More Than One Sabbath in a Week

A key clue comes in the fact that certain other festival days could also be called "Sabbaths" by first-century Jews. As Sabbaths, they also would have their days of preparation. This means that, more often than not, there could be two Sabbaths in one week, the festival Sabbath (in this case the Passover Sabbath), and the regular weekly Sabbath. If we look carefully, we can find evidence for this. The gospel of John suggests that the week Jesus dies there are two Sabbaths.

> *Now it was the day of Preparation, and the next day was*
> *to be a special Sabbath. (John 19:31a)*

John's rendering suggests that the special Sabbath is not the weekly Sabbath. Our question becomes on which day this special Sabbath might fall the year that Jesus is crucified.

Once we realize that we may have two Sabbaths in the week, this means we may have two separate days of preparation. Instead of requiring Friday to be the day of preparation for the Passover Sabbath, it could be Thursday (with Passover on Friday), or it could be Wednesday (with Passover on Thursday). A Thursday crucifixion results in three nights in the tomb, Thu-Fri-Sat, but not a full three days, since Jesus must leave the tomb no later than about 5 a.m. in the morning for the women to find it empty around dawn. A Wednesday crucifixion allows for four nights in the tomb, Wed-Thu-Fri-Sat, which is too many.

Drilling down in the gospel accounts of the empty tomb, we find that those accounts do not claim that Jesus *necessarily rose* on Sunday morning. All four gospels claim that the women find the tomb empty, and two of them claim that the women encounter Jesus in a personal appearance that morning (see main book, chapters 1 and 2).

One exception is the addendum to the gospel of Mark, which claims that Jesus rose on our Sunday, "the first day of the week" (Mk 16:9–16). As noted before (chapter 2), this addendum is missing in the early manuscripts of the gospel of Mark, and demonstrably is written in a different style. It also summarizes findings from the three other gospels about the appearances of Jesus, obviously endeavoring to bring Mark's ending into alignment with the other gospels. It is a laudable effort, but plainly a later addition. The author is not identified, and the section is not to be considered authoritative on the level of the original manuscript.

The Extended-Stay Option Offers an Alternative Time Frame

Once we see that Jesus does not necessarily rise on Sunday morning, then a Wednesday crucifixion is admissible.[45] It entails that Jesus indeed rises on or right after the third *full* day, which would be late afternoon Saturday at twilight. This time frame guarantees that he spends three full days and three full nights in the tomb. Jesus then is *recognized* in his appearances on Sunday,

---

[45] It should be noted that most scholars stick with the traditional "weekend-stay" view. They consider the 72-hour requirement too literal, despite the added issues of the *"after three days"* gospel grammar, and the spice puzzle, as described shortly. See for example, Richard L. Niswonger *New Testament History* (Grand Rapids, MI: Zondervan, 1988), 167–68.

but he already may have been raised to life well before Sunday at twilight on Saturday.[46] (What is on the schedule of Jesus between twilight and Sunday morning is unaccounted for, though some surmise this could be the interim when Jesus preaches to people long dead, as reported in 1 Pet. 3:18–20.) Instead of the weekend-stay scenario, this creates what we can term an "extended-stay" timeline. The time elapsed in the tomb extends to a full 72-hour period, congruent with the sign of Jonah that Jesus applies to himself.

If we return to our range of four possible years for the crucifixion and resurrection, in our two other non-Friday years, AD 31 and 32, is there a year when the 14th of Nisan (the day of preparation) falls on a Wednesday, with the 15th of Nisan (the Passover) falling on a Thursday?

In fact there is. Not in AD 32, where it falls on Monday (our April 14). Yet it does appear in our last option. In AD 31, the 14th of Nisan falls on Wednesday, with the Passover the next day, on Thursday. In this scenario, the day of the crucifixion of Jesus corresponds on our calendar to April 25, AD 31. In turn, that pinpoints the resurrection at twilight on Saturday, April 28, and the discovery by the women of the empty tomb, followed by the first appearances of Jesus as risen, on April 29, AD 31.[47]

Comparing Weekend-Stay Versus Extended-Stay Timelines

The extended-stay timeline provides an alternative to the weekend-stay timeline for the cross and the resurrection. Now let's assess these two timelines along at least four dimensions.

---

[46] F.A. Larson, "Part 3: The Day of the Cross," bethlehemstar.com, *The Star of Bethlehem*, see entry by Rori, 25 July 2013. Note that the author and researcher F.A. Larson is on record as favoring AD 33 for the year of Jesus's birth, though he hosts a website that welcomes discussion of a wide range of opinions.

[47] "Crucifixion Passover Date," USNO.

The Jesus-Jonah Connection

First, the extended-stay timeline has the advantage of covering the complete 72-hour duration, conforming to the sign of Jonah. Jesus emphasizes this sign, with two gospels reporting it. When Jonah was such an unreliable, cantankerous character, normally a writer would not compare him to the hero Messiah, due to the historical criterion of "embarrassment" (see main book, addition 3; and for more on the way Jesus interprets the sign of Jonah and applies it to himself, see chapters 3 and 9). Speaking from a historical viewpoint, it is highly probable that the Jonah comparison traces back to Jesus himself.

The Matter of the Emmaus Mourning

Secondly, there is the issue of what may be called "the Emmaus mourning," a challenge for the extended-stay timeline. The two travelers really are in mourning (see the beginning of chapter 9). They feel a glimmer of hope due to the news brought by the women who went to the tomb. They report that the body of Jesus is missing, but he is nowhere to be found.

> "... we had hoped that he was the one who was going to redeem Israel. And what is more, it is the third day since all this took place." (Luke 24:21)

This Emmaus walkabout occurs on the seventh day of the Jewish week, our Sunday. The comment *"it is the third day since"* could be construed to count from Friday, if parts of days are counted. This way part of Friday, all of Saturday and part of Sunday make it the third day since Jesus died. If the travelers absolutely mean the third day since the crucifixion, that would tend to contradict a Wednesday execution. Counting from Wednesday would make Sunday the fourth day since Jesus died. This sequence would favor the weekend-stay timeline. Yet the traveler is not quite that specific, saying it is the third day since *"all this"* happened. The term *"all this"* could include the priests going to Pilate and gaining permission to post a guard at the tomb on the day after the execution and burial, on Thursday. If the guards are included, then the clock could start at their posting. Then the elapsed time virtually would be a full three days since the guards were posted to the time when the travelers make their calculation.

A Gospel Grammar Lesson on "The Third Day"

The Emmaus mourning raises the question of the difference between the terms *"on the third day"* and *"after three days,"* both cropping up in the gospels. This is our third issue, turning on grammar. We have seen how Jesus predicts his own death and resurrection during his journey with his disciples to Jerusalem, at three different junctures (see chapter 3). In each of the three predictions recounted by Mark, Jesus uses the term *"after three days"* (Mk 8:31, 9:31) or *"three days later"* (Mk 10:33–34). On the other hand, Luke consistently uses the term *"on the third day"* in the three predictions by Jesus (Lk 9:22, 18:33), as well as in other situations (Lk 24:7, 24:46). In the three Jerusalem journey predictions, Matthew aligns with Luke, using *"on the third day"* (Mt 16:21, 17:23, 20:19). However, in Matthew's uniquely reported account of Pilate and the priests setting a guard at the tomb, the priests quote Jesus as saying *"After three days I will rise again"* (Mt 27:63). One would expect the enemies of Jesus to cut through the clutter and know precisely how long they need the guard stationed there to prevent any break-in at the tomb—or breakout. Thus this guard account favors the 72-hour extended-stay timeline.

When the term *"after three days"* is unambiguous, while *"on the third day"* is ambiguous, the nod would tend to go to the longer duration. Semantics aside, let us keep in mind we are dealing with Greek grammar here. The original witnesses along with Jesus spoke Aramaic, and there may have been no nuance in the original language.

The Spice Puzzle, A Case Involving Contradictory Clues

Besides the Jonah connection, the Emmaus mourning, and the gospel grammar lesson, a fourth issue must be addressed, suitably termed "the spice puzzle." The puzzle exists because of two gospel verses, one in Mark and one in Luke.

> *When the Sabbath was over, Mary Magdalene, Mary the mother of James, and Salome bought spices so that they might go to anoint Jesus's body. (Mark 16:1)*

> *Then they went home and prepared spices and perfumes. But they rested on the Sabbath in obedience to the commandment. (Luke 23:56)*

On the surface, the puzzle comes when Mark portrays them buying spices after the Sabbath is over, and Luke depicts them preparing the spices, before the Sabbath occurs. Which is it, before or after?

We know that the first two of the three women Mark mentions watch while Joseph of Arimathea places the body of Jesus in the tomb right at twilight, before the Passover meal begins. It is hard to see how they could buy spices, as Mark contends they did, before the Sabbath when it began right away. Luke says they go home and prepare spices, so perhaps they have some in stock at home already. Yet preparing spices would be considered work and would not be allowed on the Sabbath. Once the Sabbath ends Saturday at twilight in this scenario, they could prepare the spices they already possessed. But were there any spice stores open at that hour in the dark to allow them to purchase more spices? The sequence seems forced in the time allowed by the weekend-stay timeline.

Now let's see how the extended-stay timeline handles the spice puzzle. The way this timeline lays out the days, the crucifixion occurs in the afternoon on Wednesday. It is the day of preparation for the special Sabbath, the Passover, which is on Thursday.

Friday is the day of preparation for the regular weekly Sabbath, which is on Saturday. On Friday, stores would be open (probably it was more like *stalls* would be open) for purchasing provisions that would tide people over through the quiet of the Sabbath period. Lining up with Mark's account, the women could buy spices sometime Friday, *after* the *special* Sabbath Passover day on Thursday. Lining up with Luke's account, the women then could prepare the spices they bought along with any others they had in storage, later on Friday, *before* the *regular* weekly Sabbath the next day. They could have gone straight to the tomb on Friday as well; but either they run out of time, or they are in no hurry because they know the guard is posted there for three days, and they will not be given access to the body. So they align with Luke's account, resting on the regular *weekly* Sabbath. Once it ends at twilight Saturday, they are ready to go to the tomb, but rather than go in the dark they wait until they will have just enough light right at the crack of dawn.

As in the case of the sign of Jonah, the extended-stay timeline resolves the spice puzzle more effectively than the weekend-stay timeline.

Given all the information we have surveyed, we can conclude that both the weekend-stay and the extended-stay timelines are reasonable interpretations. The extended-stay version tends to have greater explanatory power. As we recognized at the outset of this discussion, these timelines may be interesting to work out, but they do not affect the reality of the resurrection event. Regardless of the duration of the elapsed time Jesus stays in the tomb, the important thing to the witnesses is that he does not stay in there for long—before he reappears to them alive in bodily form, triumphantly showing them his scars from the nails and the spear.

RESOURCE

屮

RESOURCE 4

REVIEWING RABBINIC TAKES ON THE SERVANT IN ISAIAH

For centuries many rabbis have wrestled with the meaning of Isaiah 53. Two main views diverge markedly. First we consider the view that Isaiah the prophet is speaking of Israel as a nation, using the figure or metaphor of a servant. In other words, an individual servant described in the text embodies the group or nation. Secondly, we consider the view of other rabbis that the servant is an actual individual, and likely a messianic figure.

First View: The Servant Symbolizes the Nation of Israel

The first rabbinic view asserts that the prophet is not speaking of an individual messianic figure, but is speaking of Israel as a group of people or as a nation, using the *figure* of an individual. Some emend the view that he is speaking only of a *righteous remnant* of Israel, not Israel as a whole, but still describing a *group* of people.[48] The interpretation turns on who is speaking about whom, and about what God is doing in the scenario.

> *Who has believed our message*
> *and to whom has the arm of the Lord been revealed?*
> *(Isaiah 53:1)*

Some rabbis say these are the kings of the earth speaking. The kings have despised and rejected Israel. They are waking up to the unnerving fact that Israel will be delivered by the power of the Lord, despite Israel's intense suffering at their hands.

> *Surely he took up our pain*
> *and bore our suffering,*
> *Yet we considered him punished by God,*
> *stricken by him, and afflicted. (Isaiah 53:4)*

The nations had believed that Israel had been abandoned by its God. Now according to this interpretation, the nations realize and confess that they are the *cause* of the terrible suffering Israel has endured.

> *But he was pierced for our transgressions,*
> *he was crushed for our iniquities. (Isaiah 53:5)*

Israel is the one suffering, as a result of the transgressions and iniquities of the nations (not due to its own shortcomings). The rabbis assert that the word *"for"* our transgressions, should

---

[48] For sources on this servant-figure definition in academic discussion, see J. Alec Motyer, *The Prophecy of Isaiah* (Downers Grove, IL: InterVarsity Press, 1993), 14–15. Motyer looks at the Isaiah text holistically, apart from the multiple authorship question. He detects three clear Messianic portraits in three chapter sections: King (1–37), Servant (38–55) and Anointed Conqueror (56–66). Interestingly, he writes (page 13): "The 'Messianic enigma' evidenced in the Old Testament is especially prominent in these three portraits with their implication of a Messiah who is plainly man and truly God."

be rendered *"because of"* our transgressions. Israel is suffering because the nations of the earth mistreat Israelites, perpetrating against them invasions and exiles and persecutions and massacres. But in the messianic era, Israel will be delivered and rewarded, astounding the earthly kings who hated and rejected the Jewish people.

> *Therefore I will give him a portion among the great,*
> *and he will divide the spoils with the strong.*
> *(Isaiah 53:12)*

The poem's basic motif of suffering and humiliation transforming into vindication and exaltation seems to fit with the nation's history. They suffer exile in Babylon but see in Isaiah's prophecies the promise of being raised up as the world capital in a future epoch.

The context of Isaiah seems to invite the interpretation of the single figure representing a group. Israel is called *"Daughter Zion"* in Isaiah 52:2, a singular figure symbolizing the nation. Paging further back in the book, Israel is called out as a servant.

> *"But you, Israel, my servant,*
> *Jacob, whom I have chosen,*
> *you descendants of Abraham my friend,*
> *I took you from the ends of the earth,*
> *from its farthest corners I called you.*
> *I said, 'You are my servant';*
> *I have chosen you and have not rejected you."*
> *(Isaiah 41:8–9)*

Other verses in Isaiah continue the terminology of the people of Israel as the servant of God (Isa. 44:1–2, 45:4), as well as a few verses in Jeremiah (Jer. 30:10, 46:27–28).

Several vital issues arise however, undermining the view that this section (Isa. 52:13–53:12) is really talking about a group while using an individual figure.

First, the suffering leads to *death*. *"For he was cut off from the land of the living"* (Isa. 53:8) and, if there be any doubt, *"He was assigned a grave with the wicked"* (Isa. 53:9). Despite unimaginable suffering and several grievous holocausts, the Jewish race never has died out. One of the most remarkable qualities of Israel is the way it has survived and never ceased to be a people throughout the ages.

Second, Isaiah writes *"for the transgression of my people he was punished"* (Isa. 53:8). The prophet Isaiah (or succeeding prophets, in the view that sees a second and/or third Jewish prophetic writer) would not identify as his people the nations of the earth. Isaiah would identify with Israel, especially when so much of the book is about the glorious return from exile in Babylon.

Third, the figure is described as virtually sinless. *"He had done no violence, nor was any deceit in his mouth"* (Isa. 53:9). This would not be the case for an entire people, nor even for a righteous remnant.[49]

Fourth, the individual interpretation fits with three other passages in Isaiah called "servant songs" (originally delineated by German theologian Bernhard Duhm in 1892). Our passage is the fourth of four servant songs with the other three interspersed in the preceding ten chapters: Isa. 42:1-4, 49:1-6, 50:4-9, 52:13-53:12. The first three songs would seem to view the servant as an individual. In the first, he is an agent of justice, a king, who nevertheless rules gently for *"a bruised reed he will not break"* (Isa. 42:3). In the second song, he is highly conscious of the calling he was given while in utero, to restore the nation of Israel. The calling then is expanded to include non-Jewish peoples.

> *And now the Lord says—*
> *He who formed me in the womb to be his servant*
> *to bring Jacob back to him*
> *and gather Israel to himself,*
> *for I am honored in the eyes of the Lord*
> *and my God has been my strength—*

---

[49] Efraim Goldstein, "Who's the Subject of Isaiah 53? You Decide!" n.d., jewsforjesus.org, *Jews for Jesus*, retrieved 12 July 2016.

he says:
"It is too small a thing for you to be my servant
to restore the tribes of Jacob
and bring back those of Israel I have kept.
I will also make you a light for the Gentiles,
That my salvation may reach to the ends of the earth."
(Isaiah 49:5–6)

In this second song clearly the servant is not Israel, because the servant is the one bringing Israel back to God, before reaching out to the nations.

In the third song, the servant keeps his ears open to God's truth but faces brutal opposition. Refusing to be dissuaded, he is beaten, abused, mocked and spat upon (this is likely the passage that informed Jesus when he predicted to his disciples that he would undergo this abuse, see chapter 3 in the main book). Charges are brought against him as if on trial. Yet ultimately he evades disgrace and condemnation because *"it is the Sovereign Lord who helps me"* (Isa. 50:9).

A fifth and most important issue with the group interpretation is that it runs into repeated cycles within the prophetic poetry that portray the servant as an *atoning* or *substitute* sacrifice. In this fourth song, the servant does not merely suffer at the hands of perpetrators. The suffering has a particular purpose.

Surely he took up our pain and bore our suffering,
yet we considered him punished by God,
stricken by him, and afflicted.
But he was pierced for our transgressions
he was crushed for our iniquities;
the punishment that brought us peace was on him,
and by his wounds we are healed.
We all, like sheep, have gone astray,
Each of us has turned to our own way;
and the Lord has laid on him
the iniquity of us all. (Isaiah 53:4–6)

As noted earlier, the word *"for"* our transgressions can be interpreted as *"because of"* to mean that because of the Gentile nations' persecution of Israel the Jewish people are made to suffer. However, the drumbeat rhythm of the poem uses additional terms to describe an atoning sacrifice. The servant *"took up"* or *"bore"* our suffering, and the punishment or iniquity was *"on him."* These terms taken together resonate with the tone of sacrificial language. Then verse 10 condenses the prior phrasing into an unmistakable image.

> Yet it was the Lord's will to crush him and cause him
> to suffer,
> and though the Lord makes his life an offering for sin,
> he will see his offspring and prolong his days,
> and the will of the Lord will prosper in his hand.
> (Isaiah 53:10)

The pivotal phrase *"the Lord makes his life an offering for sin"* or *"guilt offering"* makes this clear: the servant is dying for the sins of others, as a spotless ram or lamb might be put to death as a symbolic substitute for human sin in the temple sacrificial system (Lev. 5:14–19, 7:1–5). Israel as a nation may undergo punishment by God for its own ways in an effort to bring about repentance. It also may face undeserved persecution and suffering at the hands of enemy nations just for being the chosen people of God. Nevertheless, Israel as a nation is *not* given the role of *redeemer*, or redemptive suffering, that somehow pays for the sins of others.

Essentially, this work of substitution is the work of a specially designated redeemer. The redeemer's righteousness absorbs the guilt of others and his unjust death atones for their guilt. This role and title God always reserves for himself (Isa. 44:23, 48:17–20, 49:7). God redeems the nation Israel (also called *"Jacob,"* as the prophet does in fact use the singular name of the forefather Jacob for Israel as a whole in passages where God is redeeming Israel, see Isa. 44:23, 48:20). In so doing, God enlarges his redeeming work to the other nations. Always, it is God who remains the redeemer of all. He does not make Israel as a human collective the redeemer of themselves or of other nations. This condition holds in Isaiah and in the Psalms.

> *Israel, put your hope in the Lord,*
> *for with the Lord is unfailing love*
> *and with him is full redemption.*
> *He himself will redeem Israel*
> *from all their sins. (Psalm 130:7–8)*

A sixth issue with the group theory is that the servant regains life after being killed. As we saw above, Israel as a nation never has been utterly cut off and destroyed, despite many attempts by hostile, evil rulers, including the twentieth-century holocaust that caused the deaths of six million Jewish people. The servant figure in Isaiah is killed, yet then returns to life.

> *After he has suffered,*
> *he will see the light of life*
> *and be satisfied. (Isaiah 53:11)*

As Israel never was destroyed, so it would not make sense that Israel as a collective whole would be said to be brought back to life from the dead, in this context of suffering and death. Yet it would make sense to say this about an individual, even in the Old Testament context, apart from the New Testament.[50]

---

[50] J. Alec Motyer, *Isaiah*, 440–41. Motyer comments on Isa. 53:10–11: "The guilt offering has been made; what remains now is the gathering of family (all those for whom the reparation was made) and the Servant lives on, vested with authority to see that this is done. The Old Testament testifies uniformly that the dead are alive, and in this sense it is no surprise to find the Servant alive after death. But things are said about him after death that set him apart from all others. Jacob, for example, 'sees his children' (29:23) like the Servant 'sees his seed' (10c), but Jacob does so as a mere watcher from the sidelines of history. Not so the Servant! He who was crushed under the will of the Lord lives as the executor of that will ... death ushers

Second View: Some Rabbis See an Individual in Isaiah

In the face of reasons like these six, other rabbis have interpreted this fourth servant song as indeed a messianic prophecy. They see it as predicting that an individual person will fulfill this harrowing journey of suffering. Actually, this second interpretation has predominated throughout much of Jewish history. (Note that the servant-as-Israel theory does not seem to have gained traction until after the first millennia, through Rabbi Shlomo Itzchaki, also known as Rashi, AD 1040–1105.)[51] When the rabbis acknowledge an individual figure, they face the age-old contradiction. How on one hand can there be a suffering Messiah in this passage and on the other hand a warrior king Messiah in many other prophetic passages?

Traditionally, rabbis solve this with a "two-messiah" theory. This theory goes back to the Babylonian Talmud, circa AD 500. It is based on rabbinic and apocryphal writings, not any biblical texts. The first messiah is known as Messiah ben Joseph (from the half tribe of Ephraim, the son of Joseph). The second messiah is known as Messiah ben David. Ben Joseph will suffer in the "Gog Magog" war, spelled out in detail in Ezekiel 38–39. He will fight valiantly but meet his death in battle. Later, Messiah ben David will come and fight the nations victoriously, raise ben Joseph from the dead, and usher in the new epoch of world peace under his rule from Jerusalem.

With only that brief explanation, it is clear that Messiah ben Joseph does not adequately fit the figure in Isaiah 53. The figure portrayed by Isaiah is not warlike. He agrees to go to his death *"like a lamb to the slaughter."* He is eliminated through *"oppression and judgment,"* implying a legal process, not a battlefield debacle. In him is *"no violence,"* unlike a warrior, who must be violent to defend an army and triumph over an enemy (Isa. 53:7–9).

---

him into sovereign dignity and power, with his own hand administering the saving purposes of the Lord, and as victor taking the spoil ..."

[51] Rachmiel Frydland, "The Rabbi's Dilemma: A look at Isaiah 53," n.d., jewsforjesus.org, *Jews for Jesus*, retrieved 12 July 2016.

While this two-messiah theory does not explain adequately the figure in Isaiah 53, it must be noted that it edges closer to the Christian position. That position holds to a single messiah, but with two separate missions. This is how Peter clarifies the two missions in his preaching at the temple plaza, when the people ask him what they should do about their mistake in crucifying Jesus.

> *"Now, fellow Israelites, I know that you acted in ignorance, as did your leaders. But this is how God fulfilled what he had foretold through all the prophets, saying that his Messiah would suffer. Repent then, and turn to God, so that your sins may be wiped out, that times of refreshing may come from the Lord, and that he may send the Messiah, who has been appointed for you—even Jesus. Heaven must receive him until the time comes for God to restore everything, as he promised long ago through his holy prophets." (Acts 3:17–21)*

The upcoming return, on the part of this same Jesus who was crucified and raised, is signaled by other NT writers (Mk 13:26; Jn 21:22–23; 1 Pet. 1:3–5; Heb. 9:28; 1 Thess. 1:10; Titus 2:13; James 5:7; Jude 1:21). Essentially and in a way ironically, in view of Peter's preaching and the OT prophets, Christians today are awaiting and anticipating the same type of powerful, politically triumphant Messiah as are traditional Jewish believers. This irony was not lost on a modern rabbi. He once was heard to say that when the Messiah comes, and if his name does indeed turn out to be Jesus (or *Yeshua*), then he—the rabbi—will be the first in line to get baptized.

RESOURCE

RESOURCE 5

SURVEYING JEWISH EXPECTATIONS OF RESURRECTION

---

aul is in the hot seat at the Sanhedrin. This group
customarily comprised of 71 members, the governing
council in Jerusalem, stands united against him. They
are ready to condemn him to death for asserting that
Jesus was raised from the dead and that he is their Jewish Messiah,
whom they or their forebears rejected almost three decades ago.

A Convenient Jewish Divide Over the Future Resurrection

Just in time, Paul hits upon an escape path. First, he identifies
himself with one sub-group of the council, the Pharisees.
Secondly, he redefines the issue at hand, which happens to be
the charge against him.

> *Then Paul, knowing that some of them were Sadducees
> and others Pharisees, called out in the Sanhedrin, "My
> brothers, I am a Pharisee, descended from Pharisees. I*

*stand on trial because of the hope of the resurrection of
the dead." (Acts 23:6)*

Paul changes the specific charge of whether he is claiming that
Jesus was raised from the dead, to the general charge of whether
anyone who is dead can be raised. He knows exactly what he is
doing. He sets the two political/theological parties against each
other. The Pharisee contingent takes his side and declares him
innocent. The other side, the Sadducees who run the temple system,
want Paul dead and gone. The group gets violent. The Roman
troops have to intervene. For his own protection, they sweep Paul
away to the nearby barracks called the Antonia Fortress where the
soldiers are quartered. Outwitting his accusers by dividing them,
Paul wins the day—or at least a two-year sabbatical, as things turn
out, in cushy confinement in a palace on the coast (see chapter 6).
What is the reason why Paul was able to divide the council and
escape? Parenthetically, Luke tells us in his account.

*(The Sadducees say that there is no resurrection, and
that there are neither angels nor spirits, but the Pharisees
believe all these things.) (Acts 23:8)*

About thirty years previously, Jesus too had earned the
hostility of both groups, the Pharisees and the Sadducees. Shortly
before his death, while he taught on the temple grounds, both
groups approached him with trick questions. They want to make
him look foolish in front of the crowds, hoping to drive people
away from him. First, the Pharisees come at him with the question
of paying taxes to Caesar. He eludes their trap, only to have the
Sadducees come at him with a question about the afterlife (which
they believe is mere fantasy, simple wishful thinking). They spin
a scenario about a woman who has seven husbands on earth (Mk
12:18–23). Whose husband will she be in heaven, they snarkily
inquire? Jesus answers the question directly, then catches them
off-guard by challenging their hidden premise—that there is no
resurrection of the dead.

Jesus replied, "Are you not in error because you do not know the Scriptures or the power of God? When the dead rise, they will neither marry nor be given in marriage; they will be like the angels in heaven. Now about the dead rising—have you not read in the Book of Moses, in the account of the burning bush, how God said to him, 'I am the God of Abraham, the God of Isaac, and the God of Jacob'? He is not the God of the dead, but of the living. You are badly mistaken!" (Mark 12:24–27)

Jesus logically concludes that God would not name himself after the patriarchs if they were not very much alive in a resurrected state. He soundly rebukes the Sadducees for their ignorance of scripture (Ex. 3:6). Their sect claimed to accept as authoritative only the first five books of the OT, the Torah or Pentateuch, attributed to Moses. Jesus ingeniously proves from within their own limited scripture range that they are wrong about the resurrection in the end times.

To be sure, other than the passage Jesus interprets, there is not much material about the last-days resurrection in the first five OT books. (Enoch is taken away without dying after walking faithfully with God throughout his 365 years. But this is the exception for one individual, not the rule for a group, and technically does not involve either death or resurrection, only ascension, in Gen. 5:24 and Heb. 11:5. Similar is the account of the ascension of the prophet Elijah in 2 Kings 2:1, 11.) The OT anticipation of a group resurrection at the end of the age comes primarily through the writings of the prophets and the psalms. For the Pharisees and Sadducees, the difference in their views of authoritative writings may account for their vicious divergence of opinion on whether people will be raised from the dead. Even among those who believed there would be a resurrection in the last days, there was disagreement over who might be raised.

In this brief survey of Jewish expectations of a future resurrection, we will look first at several representative OT passages, then at a few Jewish writings outside the Bible.

Credit goes to the scholar George Eldon Ladd for much of this discussion.[52] Having this context at hand helps determine what the disciples meant when they claimed that Jesus had been resurrected from the dead.

Views on the Afterlife from the Old Testament

The book of Psalms includes a variety of authors who believe in an afterlife. Their focus is on their connection with God. The psalmists express a confidence that their communion with God will go on; it will not end with this life but continue eternally.

The psalmist David, known even more for serving as Israel's most faithful king, foresees life with God after death.

> *Surely your goodness and love will follow me*
> *all the days of my life,*
> *and I will dwell in the house of the Lord forever.*
> *(Psalm 23:6, by David)*

Another psalmist, Asaph, is probably one of three members of the tribe of Levi whom David appoints to lead worship. Later, he is selected to perform at the dedication of the temple built by Solomon (1 Chron. 6:39, 2 Chron. 5:12). Asaph absolutely sees life continuing forever, despite his body expiring.

> *You guide me with your counsel,*
> *and afterward you will take me into glory.*
> *Whom have I in heaven but you?*
> *And earth has nothing I desire besides you.*
> *My flesh and my heart may fail,*

---

[52] George Eldon Ladd, *I Believe in the Resurrection* (Grand Rapids, MI: Wm. B. Eerdmans, 1975). See two other excellent sources on the Jewish view of the resurrection at the end of the age: Jon Levenson, *Resurrection and the Restoration of Israel: The Ultimate Victory of the God of Life* (New Haven, CT: Yale University Press, 2008), and N.T. Wright, *The Resurrection of the Son of God* (Minneapolis, MN: Fortress Press, 2003).

but God is the strength of my heart
and my portion forever. (Psalm 73:24–26, by Asaph)

Another psalmist is sure that after death God will not abandon his people if they are upright, unlike those who *"trust in themselves"* (Ps. 49:13).

They are like sheep and are destined to die;
death will be their shepherd
(but the upright will prevail over them in the morning).
Their forms will decay in the grave,
far from their princely mansions.
But God will redeem me from the realm of the dead;
He will surely take me to himself.
(Psalm 49:14–15, by the Sons of Korah)

The psalmists hold confident hope that life will not end in death but continue beyond it. Yet they leave it somewhat ambiguous whether this eternal communion with God will be continued in bodily form.

When the prophets weigh in, they tend to be more specific about a physical resurrection. Isaiah, in a passage about the end times, says the Lord Almighty *"will swallow up death forever"* (Isa. 25:8, also quoted by Paul in his description of the future group resurrection in 1 Cor. 15:54, see addition 4 in the main book). Shortly afterward in Isaiah, those who belong to the Lord are promised a bodily resurrection.

But your dead will live, Lord;
their bodies will rise —
let those who dwell in the dust
wake up and shout for joy —
your dew is like the dew of the morning;
the earth will give birth to her dead. (Isaiah 26:19)

There is a famous vision of a valley of dry human bones recounted by the prophet Ezekiel (Ezek. 37:1–14). Suddenly with a blast of divine power the bones form into skeletons that stand, are clothed with flesh, and animated to life with breath. While this vivid scene may allude to the future resurrection of the righteous, in context, it seems focused on the re-gathering of the nation Israel to come alive to God spiritually, rather than a prediction of the end-times resurrection.

However, another prophet, Daniel, predicts a bodily resurrection in no uncertain terms. He foresees a bodily resurrection not only of the righteous but also of the unrighteous.

> *"Multitudes who sleep in the dust of the earth will awake: some to everlasting life, others to shame and everlasting contempt." (Daniel 12:2)*

Along with this prediction for the group resurrection, Daniel relates a final vignette. In a vision, *"a man clothed in linen"* gives him personal assurance that he will be raised from the dead.

> *"As for you, go your way till the end. You will rest, and then at the end of the days you will rise to receive your allotted inheritance." (Daniel 12:13)*

In the OT, there are psalmists and prophets who definitely foresee life with God continuing after death. Some specifically indicate a future bodily resurrection of those who belong to God. Some of them note as well that the unrighteous will be raised, but their fate will not be pleasant.

Resurrection Views from Outside the Old Testament

Looking outside the biblical texts to other Jewish literature, our survey finds some other views on what the future resurrection entails. In the book of Enoch (no relation to the Enoch in Gen. 5:21–24), written by an unknown author in the second or first century BC, multiple views are offered. The Enoch character encounters sinful persons in *"Sheol,"* a term also used in the OT for the realm of the dead. It carries the idea of an intermediate state, or "waiting zone," before final judgment. In this book, these sinful persons better not get their hopes up, for they will not be raised but slain in the day of judgment (Enoch 22:13). In another section, the righteous will be raised but the unrighteous will not be (Enoch 46:6, 51:1–2). The righteous will definitely remain in bodily form, for they will eat, lie down and get up repeatedly, and their *"garments shall not grow old"* (Enoch 62:13–16). In a later part in Enoch, the writer uses figurative language that may or may not entail resurrection in bodily form; if this viewpoint sees resurrection only in spirit, this would be a rare instance in Jewish thought (Enoch 104:2).

Another book written near the time of the Enoch writings (180 BC) takes a dimmer view of the afterlife. The book is *Ecclesiasticus*, by a known author, Jesus son of Sirach (hence his book is sometimes called *The Wisdom of Jesus*, but here we will refer to him as Sirach). He sees no future life beyond the domain of Sheol. His description explains why David could be so freaked out by the thought that he might be stuck there permanently (see Ps.16:10, 30:3, 86:13). To Sirach, Sheol is dark (22.11), silent (17.27–28), and a place where you cannot praise God (18.28). Sheol offers no pleasures (14.16), induces endless sleep (46.19), and there is no coming back from it (38.21). Obviously, the Sadducees shared the nihilistic mind-set of Sirach.

On a somewhat brighter note, the Maccabean martyrs cannot abide the sulkiness of Sirach. Written around the same time (circa second century BC), 2 Maccabees gives a historical account of the severe persecution of Jews by the Greek ruler Antiochus Epiphanes. In this book, the twin hopes of bodily resurrection and final vindication by God are prominent (2 Maccabees 7:9, 11, 14, 22–33, 29).

From this brief survey, we can draw a few conclusions about the definitions of resurrection that were in the Jewish tradition at the time of the disciples.

- In the Jewish psalms, the fear of Sheol was real, for it meant being cast into a waiting zone where one might not return. However, those communing with God were pretty sure that he would find a way to keep them alive in relationship to himself.
- There is hope of a resurrection in the body for the righteous in the OT, mainly in the psalms and prophets; but Jesus manages to find it as well in the Torah, or books of Moses, much to the dismay of the Sadducees.
- Other Jewish writings carry the hope of future resurrection. They assume that it will be a group resurrection in the end times, with bodies that are transformed to one degree or another.

Like the Pharisees, the disciples probably held the hope that they would be raised with the righteous in the end times. They had the category in their minds that those resurrected from the dead would still have bodies, rather than become disembodied spirits, in a future group resurrection. This assumption is dramatized in an episode recorded in the gospel of John, where Jesus discusses this belief with his friend and frequent host, Martha. Her brother Lazarus has died, but Jesus tells her that he will rise again. Underwhelmed, she tells him that is not exactly breaking news.

> Martha answered, "I know he will rise again in the resurrection at the last day." (John 11:24)

In his reply, Jesus informs her that he himself is the power behind anyone who is raised to life.

> Jesus said to her, "I am the resurrection and the life. The one who believes in me will live, even though they die; and whoever lives by believing in me will never die. Do you believe this?" (John 11:25–26)

Jesus challenges her to put her faith in him. To validate that faith and to display that power, she will see her brother rise not just in the last days, but right in that hour. This resurrection of her brother would be different than the resurrection of Jesus that shortly she would see (assuming she would mingle with the disciples during the forty days when Jesus made appearances). Although raised by Jesus back to life on earth, her brother would die again, and await the resurrection she knew would come, as she told Jesus, on the last day. In contrast, Jesus in his resurrected body would ascend directly to heaven to be exalted and to rule from heaven, pending his return to mop up the mess on earth, according to the disciples' reports as recorded by Luke in Acts (1:9, 2:33–36, 3:21).

While the disciples likely believed in an end-times resurrection where the righteous would have bodies, they had to sort through what it meant that Jesus had been raised in his body individually, in advance.

Why him?
Why now?
Where are the rest of the righteous persons who are supposed to be raised together?

Fifty days after Jesus rose—including a forty-day period for interactive appearances then ten days following his ascension—the disciples had made up their minds. They preached the news that because Jesus had been raised in the body here and now, and then ascended to heaven, he is the Messiah. His suffering in body and in spirit now transformed into glory, delivers human beings from sin and separation from God, if people will trust in him (Acts 2:32–39). In time he will return to catalyze the human resurrection in the last days. He will usher into the joys of eternal life with God all believers who have inhabited physical bodies, whether they be dead or alive at his coming—though spiritually and in some manner miraculously these bodies will be transformed, so that they are refitted and made suitable for eternity (1 Cor. 15:35–44).

RESOURCE

FOUND IN THE GROUND

ARCHAEOLOGICAL

INDEX

RESOURCE 6

FOUND IN THE GROUND
ARCHAEOLOGICAL INDEX

---

rchaeology is the discipline of excavating layers of earth in order to discover artifacts from past cultures. It is said that archaeology in Israel is the national pastime, due to the many sites that carry great meaning for different centuries and different faith communities. Due to the spread of the gospel message, the span of current and future relevant sites for excavation includes most of the Mediterranean area.

Here the guide provides a list of findings that corroborate to various extents our sources for the nine lines of evidence for the resurrection. The findings are presented according to the chapters where they most strongly figure. Each of the first nine chapters feature windows, or boxes, that describe applicable archaeological findings, in *brief* form. In this Found in the Ground Archaeological Index, *fuller* descriptions of each discovery are offered for those who would want more detailed information.

For each finding, I have sought when available to provide the year discovered, original location, team leader, place where it currently is kept (if not still in the ground at the site, as is often the case with ruins of buildings), and whether it confirms or supports assertions in biblical texts. Sources for each finding are included, many of them easily accessible online, often with photos. Obviously, archaeologists constantly make new findings, so this list most assuredly will be able to grow. First you will find the master list of the more than forty entries that appear in the main book and in this index. Then the guide goes chapter by chapter to supply the full descriptions with source references included.

Admittedly, it was eye-opening for me during the research for this investigation to see the high degree of evidence that has been found in the ground mainly over just the last two centuries. This work has been accomplished by diligent archaeologists—and sometimes by regular workers going about their daily jobs—from diverse nationalities and faith perspectives. As a result of the efforts from many different hands, the evidence for the reliability and trustworthiness of the New Testament authors continues to mount up.

LIST OF FINDINGS

BY CHAPTER

1:

1.1 Rock-Cut Tombs.
1.2 Anklebone from Crucified Man.
1.3 Tomb Jesus Occupied.
1.4 Pilate Inscription.
1.5 Magdala Tower, Harbor, Pools.
1.6 Magdala Synagogue and Stone.

2:

2.1 Emmaus Village.

3:

3.1 Bethsaida Village and Harbor.
3.2 Caesarea Philippi and Panias Shrine.
3.3 Pool of Siloam.
3.4 Capernaum Synagogue.
3.5 Jericho in the Time of Jesus.
3.6 Palace and Pavement Where Pilate Judged Jesus.

4:

4.1 House and Courtyard of High Priest.
4.2 Ancient Galilee Fishing Boat.
4.3 Galilee Boat Harbors.
4.4 Peter's House in Capernaum.
4.5 Bone Box of High Priest.
4.6 Italian Regiment Inscription.

5:

5.1 The Floor Where Salome Danced.
5.2 Herodian Theater or Hippodrome.
5.3 Tomb of One Philip or Another.

LIST OF FINDINGS

BY CHAPTER

6:

6.1 Temple Warning Inscriptions.

6.2 The Damascus Street Called "Straight."

6.3 Inscriptions of Cyprus Official Who Believes.

6.4 Egnatian Way.

6.5 Temple of Artemis.

6.6 Statues of Artemis.

6.7 Commercial Shops and Agora.

6.8 Riotous Theater.

6.9 Evidence for the Antonia Fortress.

6.10 Palace Where Paul Appeals to Caesar.

6.11 The Renowned Roman Road, the Appian Way.

7:

7.1 Erastus Inscription.

7.2 Gallio or Delphi Inscription.

7.3 Judgment Platform or Bema.

8:

8.1 Trumpeting Inscription.

8.2 Western Wall.

8.3 Arch of Titus South Panel Relief.

8.4 Temple Sundial.

8.5 Inscription on the Reign of David.

8.6 Rock of Abraham.

9:

9.1 Isaiah Scroll from the Cave Near the Dead Sea.

9.2 Modest House in Nazareth.

⁊:

WOMEN ARE THE FIRST WITNESSES TO THE EMPTY TOMB

FINDINGS

1.1 Rock-Cut Tombs. Jerusalem. Tombs are found outside the walls in most directions, and in surrounding towns. Some tombs trace back to the First Temple period, ninth to seventh centuries BC, showing strong Phoenician influence. The "garden tomb" (found in 1867 by Conrad Schick) is alleged by some to be the tomb that held Jesus; yet it is dated by most scholars to the First (Solomon's) Temple period, much too early to be the tomb where Jesus lay. However, it retains the best environmental ambiance for remembering and contemplating the resurrection. The later wave of rock-cut tombs date to the period from when Hasmonean rule began until the temple was destroyed (about 140 BC to AD 70). Hasmonean rule is the period of Jewish independence from Greek hegemony starting under Simon Maccabaeus in 140 BC, continuing to a degree under the Romans, then ending with Herod the Great taking the throne as a client-king of Rome in 37 BC. Usually the richer the family, the closer the tomb is to the temple mount. Among the well preserved are the tombs of Helena of Adiabene, an Assyrian queen and Jewish convert, buried in the early AD 50s; the tomb of Jason, believed to be a Jewish naval commander; and the tomb of Nicanor, an upscale door maker. The tombs confirm that the burial practice undergone by the body of Jesus as described in the gospels was indeed in fashion during his time. (Mk 15:46; Mt 27:59–60; Lk 23:53; Jn 19:41–42.)

- Jodi Magness, "What Did Jesus' Tomb Look Like?" in Hershel Shanks and Ellen White, eds., *Jesus & Archaeology* (Wash., DC: Biblical Archaeology Society, 2016), 80–83.

1.2 Anklebone from Crucified Man. Jerusalem. Found in 1968 by Greek-born Vassilios Tzaferis. Kept in Israel Museum, Jerusalem. Among the many bone boxes (ossuaries) found in tombs around Jerusalem was the box of an individual named *Yehohanan, son of Hagkol.* In it were bones from several family members. One bone was unique, because it had a 4.5 in. or 11.5 cm iron nail thrust through it. The nail indicated the individual had been crucified. Usually, iron nails were pried from victims in order to be recycled. This nail bent and could not be extracted. Detailed investigations found traces of olive wood on the nail, indicating that when it had been hammered it had bent at a knot in the wood. The finding confirms that Jewish law permitted burial of crucified persons with honor in regular family tombs, if the violation was against secular Roman law, not Jewish law. This discovery definitively debunks the theory that Jesus had to be buried in a trench or a mass grave. It supports the gospel accounts of the tomb burial of Jesus. (Mk 15:45–46; Lk 23:53; Mt 27:59–60; Jn 19:40–42.)

- Clyde E. Fast and Mitchell G. Reddish, *Lost Treasures of the Bible – Understanding the Bible Through Archaeological Artifacts in World Museums* (Grand Rapids, MI: Wm. B. Eerdmans, 2008), 318–22.

- Matti Friedman, "In a stone box, the only trace of crucifixion," timesofisrael.com, *The Times of Israel*, 26 March 2012.

- Jodi Magness, "What Did Jesus' Tomb Look Like?" in Hershel Shanks and Ellen White, eds., *Jesus & Archaeology* (Wash., DC: Biblical Archaeology Society, 2016), 80–83.

- "A Tomb in Jerusalem Reveals the History of Crucifixion and Roman Crucifixion Methods", n.a. (staff), biblicalarchaeology.org, Bible History Daily, *Biblical Archaeology Society*, 22 Jul 2011. Attached to the article is a detailed report from the archaeologist who found the ankle bone, originally published as Vassilios Tzaferis, "Crucifixion—The Archaeological Evidence," *Biblical Archaeology Review*, Jan/Feb 1985, 44–53.

1.3 Tomb Jesus Occupied. Jerusalem. Rediscovered in AD 325. Located by Helena, mother of Roman emperor Constantine, in collaboration with Jerusalem Patriarch Macarius. An elaborate Romanesque church, called "the Church of the Holy Sepulchre," was built over the site. It replaced a pagan temple of Venus built by the earlier Roman emperor Hadrian. He wanted to cover up the tomb where Jesus had been, in order to deter pilgrimages. In the center of the church rotunda, a small shrine encloses the tomb. Formerly a rock quarry, the site stood outside the walls of Jerusalem at the time of Jesus. It confirms with high probability the actual site of Joseph of Arimathea's fresh-cut tomb, as the gospels narrate. (Mk 15:45–46; Mt. 27:57–60; Lk 23:50–54; Jn 19:38–42.)

- Dan Bahat, "Does the Holy Sepulchre Church Mark the Burial of Jesus?" *Biblical Archaeology Review*, 12:3, May/June 1986.

- Gordon Govier, "Why Two Tombs Compete for Jesus' Burial," christianitytoday.com, *Christianity Today*, 30 Nov 2016.

- Jodi Magness, "What Did Jesus' Tomb Look Like?" in Hershel Shanks and Ellen White, eds., *Jesus & Archaeology* (Wash., DC: Biblical Archaeology Society, 2016), 80–83.

- "Church of the Holy Sepulchre," wikipedia.org, retrieved 6 July 2017.

1.4 Pilate Inscription. Caesarea Maritima, Israel. Found in 1961 by an Italian team led by Antonio Frova. It is a limestone plaque measuring 32 in x 25 in or 82cm x 65cm. Kept in the Israel Museum, Jerusalem. The plaque commemorates Pilate, in his title as prefect, dedicating a building to the Roman emperor at the time, Tiberius. The plaque was preserved from weather or human defacement because it had been recycled for use as a step in a staircase placed facedown, for a later theater addition. It confirms the gospel accounts of the existence and rule of Pilate during the time of Jesus, debunking notions that he is a fictional figure. (Mk 15:1–15, Jn 18:28–19:22.)

- R. Steven Notley, "Pontius Pilate Sadist or Saint?" *Biblical Archaeology Review*, Jul/Aug 2017, 40–49, 59–60.

- Jerry Vardaman, "A new inscription which mentions Pilate as 'prefect'," *Journal of Biblical Literature*, vol. 81.1 (1962), 70–71.

- "Pilate stone," wikipedia.org, retrieved 5 July 2017.

1.5 Magdala Tower, Harbor, Pools. Magdala, Galilee, Israel. Found in 2007 by Italian archaeologist Stefano De Luca. The findings included stone foundations of a tower (*migdal* is Hebrew for tower, with other names for the area the Aramaic *magdala nunaya* meaning "fish tower" or the Greek term, *magdala tarichaea* meaning "tower of fish salters"). Found along with the tower base was an L-shaped harbor basin with a breakwater, six mooring stones for boats to be secured, plus a quay or wharf for unloading and loading cargo. Near the tower were vats likely used to store fish in fresh water. The city included boulevards, public baths, a water system with wells and fountains, all with first-century layers. The site confirms that Magdala was a key port on the lakeshore for storing and transporting fish. It is likely the disciples sold fish in this area. It is possible they met and conversed with Mary Magdalene when they went about their business in this town (Lk 8:1–2).

- Jurgen K. Zangenberg, "Archaeological News from the Galilee: Tiberias, Magdala and Rural Galilee," magdalaproject.org, *Magdala Project*, 27 June 2011, retrieved 20 July 2017.

1.6 Magdala Synagogue and Stone. Magdala, Galilee, Israel. Dated to the first century AD. Found by Israelis Dina Avshalom-Gorni and Arfan Najar, on a team led by Spanish Franciscan Father Juan Solana in 2009. It is the first synagogue found in Magdala (an earlier find in the 1970s thought to be a small synagogue is now considered a latrine). The building is 1290 sq ft or 120 sq m with a capacity for about 200 people. The evidence included ornamented columns, floor mosaics, painted walls, and stone benches lining the walls. Discovered in a central spot, less than a foot under the soil, was a stone block. The block had an image carved in relief forming a seven-branched menorah bordered on either side by a vase and a column, among other reliefs. The findings confirm that synagogues are actively used in Galilee in the time of Jesus, and are not anachronisms in the gospels, as some critics once contended. It is possible though speculative that Mary Magdalene encounters Jesus at the synagogue and is healed here in her hometown. (Mk 1:39; Mt 4:23, 9:35; Lk 4:15, 44; Jn 18:20.)

- Ariel Sabar, "Unearthing the World of Jesus," smithsonianmag.com, *Smithsonian Magazine*, Jan 2016, retrieved 8 July 2017.

- Jurgen K. Zangenberg, "Archaeological News from the Galilee: Tiberias, Magdala and Rural Galilee," magdalaproject.org, *Magdala Project*, 27 June 2011, retrieved 20 July 2017.

- Marcela Zapata-Mesa, "Magdala 2016: Excavating the Hometown of Mary Magdalene," biblicalarchaeology.org, Bible History Daily, *Biblical Archaeology Society*, 8 July 2016, retrieved 20 July 2017.

2:

APPEARANCE REPORTS INVOLVE MULTIPLE WITNESSES

FINDINGS

2.1 Emmaus Village. Emmaus. The site for the village of Emmaus probably has been found, only a dispute continues over which it is among three competing sites: Emmaus-Nicopolis, Emmaus-Qubeibeh, or Emmaus Moza or Motza. Each site reflects the meaning of Emmaus, featuring a "warm spring or well." Each sits along a major ancient road. Each is at least 7 miles or 11 km (or 60 Roman stadia) away from Jerusalem, as Luke indicates (Lk 24:13). Alternative textual readings from credible ancient versions put the distance not at 60 stadia but at 160 stadia, about 18 miles or 31 km from Jerusalem, giving Nicopolis a chance for consideration. Nicopolis (found in 1852 by Edward Robinson) lies the farthest from the city, but has the earliest tradition supporting it. It is situated on a road to the coast. Qubeibeh (found circa 1940s by Bellarmino Bagatti of Studium Biblicum Franciscan) is closer in and on the road to Lydda, but not associated with NT Emmaus until AD 1290. A third alternative site is known as Moza, mentioned as Mozah, a Benjaminite village, in Joshua 18:26. Moza (found in 1881 by William F. Birch of The Palestine Exploration Fund) later known as Colonia to the Roman soldiers who retired there, lies closer in at about 36–46 stadia, or 4–5 miles or 6.5–8 km. It is on the road to Jaffa and has artifacts indicating habitation before the fall of Jerusalem. To make a round-trip walk from Jerusalem to Emmaus-Nicopolis in a single day takes longer than from the other two options but it is possible, though arduous. It takes an elapsed time of 9 hours for 15-minute miles, or 12 hours for 20-minute miles. Beyond these three sites, other candidates for Emmaus may arise.

- "Emmaus", n.a., n.d., seetheholyland.net, retrieved 13 July 2017.

- Edward Robinson, Eli Smith and Others (sic), *Later Biblical Researches in Palestine and Adjacent Regions* (London: John Murray, 1856).

- Hershel Shanks, "Emmaus Where Christ Appeared," in Hershel Shanks and Ellen White, eds., *Jesus & Archaeology* (Wash., DC: Biblical Archaeology Society, 2016), 90–101.

3:

JESUS PREDICTS HIS DEATH AND RESURRECTION

FINDINGS

3.1 Bethsaida Village and Harbor. Galilee, Israel. Northeastern shore of Jordan river. Aptly named, the village near the Sea of Galilee means "house of fishing" (or to some scholars "house of hunting"). Two sites compete for the village of Bethsaida, although they may be related as two parts of the same settlement: a lower modest one closer to the lakeside (called "el-Araj," found in 1870 by Gottlieb Schumacher), and a more refined one up the hill (called "Julias," found in 1838 by Edward Robinson). John reports Bethsaida is the hometown of three disciples, Peter, Andrew and Philip (Jn 1:44). Located on the northeastern shore near where the Jordan River enters the Sea of Galilee, Bethsaida suffers from silt built up over the centuries to the point that it now lies one mile or 1.5 km north from the lakeshore. The lower village lies close to the excavated harbor and road and it is likely the place where the disciples gather. The site supports the account of landing at Bethsaida harbor for the disciples' retreat before their journey to Jerusalem (Mk 8:13, 22). In addition, the area topography provides spacious areas of green grass with flat hills that would accommodate seating for the biblical episode of the serendipitous outdoor picnic feeding 5,000 or more people. (Mk 6:32–44; Mt 14:13–21; Lk 9:10–17; Jn 6:5–15.)

- Rami Arav, Richard A. Freund and John F. Schroder, Jr., "Bethsaida Rediscovered—Longlost City Found North of Galilee Shore," *Biblical Archaeology Review,* 26:01, Jan/Feb 2000.

- Mendel Nun, "Has the Lost City of Bethsaida Finally Been Found?" jerusalemperspective.com, 01 July 1998.

- Carl E. Savage, *Biblical Bethsaida: A Study of the First Century C.E. in Galilee* (Lanham, MD: Lexington Books, Rowman & Littlefield Publishers, 2011).

- "Bethsaida—An Ancient Fishing Village on the shore of the Sea of Galilee," Archaeological Sites No. 5, Mfa.gov. il, *Israel Ministry of Foreign Affairs,* 21 Mar 2000, retrieved 13 July 2017.

- "The El-Araj Excavation Project," emmausonline.net, *Emmaus Educational Services,* Morehead, NC, 2014, retrieved 7 July 2017.

3.2 Caesarea Philippi and Panias Shrine. Banias, Golan Heights. Site is found in 1838 by American Edward Robinson. At the bottom of the foothills of Mount Hermon, an ancient shrine developed around a spring. The spring is the source of the Banias River, a main tributary flowing into the Jordan River. The shrine honored the Greek goat-footed god Pan, a mythical figure with a broad portfolio that included forests, music, herding, hunting and victory in battle by instilling panic in the enemy. A city developed beyond the shrine which Herod the Great conquers and seizes from its Iturian inhabitants in 23 BC. His son Philip expands the city in honor of the emperor Augustus, hence the name Caesarea Philippi during the time of Jesus. Later, Herod's grandson Agrippa I is given the city by the Roman emperor Caligula. Still later Agrippa II rebuilds the city to honor his Roman emperor Nero. The location of the city and shrine supports the account of the disciples' retreat to villages on the outskirts of the city, when

Jesus poses the question of whether the crowds recognize his identity. (Mk 8:27, 9:2; Lk 3:1.)

- "Panias" and "Caesarea Philippi," wikipedia.org, retrieved 7 Jul 2017.

3.3 Pool of Siloam. Jerusalem. Found in 2004. The site was identified and further excavated by Ronny Reich and Eli Shukron. It started with two stone steps, unearthed during a city maintenance project to fix a major water pipe, south of the temple mount. The two steps led to a wider excavation that uncovered a stepped stone structure 225 ft or 69m long in a trapezoidal shape, widening on the west side facing the Tyropoean Valley. They find three rows of five steps with two landings and the flat bottom of the pool; the design allows for washing, at various volumes of water collected in the pool from its source, the Gihon Spring in the Kidron Valley. As a naturally occurring spring, it provided fresh drinking water and qualified the pool as a *mikveh* for ritual bathing. This spring was on the opposite side of the ridge from the pool, so the streaming water travels west 1750 ft or 533m through a winding underground tunnel, engineered under King Hezekiah (reigning c. 715–686 BC) as attested by OT writers (2 Kings 20:20; 2 Chron. 32:2–4, 30; Isa. 22:11). The pool configuration confirms the accuracy of the setting in the gospel of John for the account of Jesus healing a man born blind. First Jesus spits on the ground, then makes virtual mud pies, then applies the pies to the man's eyes, and finally sends him off to wash in the Pool of Siloam. After the man gains his sight, his witness to Jesus first provokes consternation, then vicious hostility, on the part of the opponents of Jesus. (Jn 9:1–12.)

- "The Siloam Pool: Where Jesus Healed the Blind Man," n.a. (staff), biblicalarchaeology.org, Bible History Daily, *Biblical Archaeology Society*, 2 Jul 2017, originally published in 2011.

- "Where is the Original Siloam Pool from the Bible?" n.a. (staff), biblicalarchaeology.org, Bible History Daily, *Biblical Archaeology Society*, 23 Jan 2017.

3.4 Capernaum Synagogue. Capernaum, Galilee, Israel. In 1866, British cartographer Charles William Wilson identifies this synagogue site, while the site of the town was discovered earlier by Edward Robinson in 1838. The synagogue, built of limestone, dates to the fourth century AD, based on coins and pottery found beneath the floor. The observed ruins however are built over a first-century AD building, with black basalt for a foundation. The finding supports the accounts of Jesus teaching in a synagogue in Capernaum, the town he selected as his base of operation. (Mk 1:21; Lk 4:31–32.)

- "Archaeology in Israel: The Synagogue at Capernaum," n.a., n.d., jewishvirtuallibrary.org, *American-Israeli Cooperative Enterprise*, retrieved 9 July 2017.

- "The Ancient Synagogue," n.a., n.d., capernaum.custodia. org, Sanctuary Capernaum, *Custodia Terrae Sanctae*, retrieved 14 July 2017.

3.5 Jericho in the Time of Jesus. Jericho, West Bank. Found by American Charles Warren in 1868. Described as a fortress town in the OT writings, Jericho in the time of Jesus functions more as a resort town for the aristocratic and priestly elites, with Herod the Great building his winter palace there. On the edge of the desert, Jericho (meaning "fragrant") is an oasis with many springs and warm weather. At the time, the economy flourishes with production and trade in date palms, wine, spices and perfumes. Only 18 miles or 29 km from Jerusalem, the city of Jericho nevertheless is difficult to reach due to the terrain. Jericho sits 820 ft or 250m below sea level, while Jerusalem rises to 2,550 ft or 777m above sea level. The road from Jericho to Jerusalem amounts to more than a 3280 ft or 1000m climb. It is an arduous and treacherous road to traverse, prowled by thieves who strike suddenly then escape into the desert. No wonder Jesus sets his parable of the Good Samaritan on this road (Lk 10:25–37). Excavations in Jericho find ruins from Herod's winter palace, hippodrome, and aqueducts. The site supports the account of the disciples' journey with Jesus through the Jordan Valley, through Jericho, then up the steep incline to Jerusalem. The site also explains the high degree of wealth obtained by one of Jesus's direct converts, Zacchaeus. He collects taxes in prosperous Jericho and, according to Luke, hosts Jesus on this final journey. (Lk 19:1–10, 28, Mk 10:46–47.)

- Maura Sala, "Road to Jericho," bibleodyssey.org, *Society of Biblical Literature*, n.d., retrieved 10 July 2017.

- "Jericho", n.a., biblebasics.co.uk, n.p., n.d., retrieved 10 July 2017.

- "Jericho," wikipedia.org, retrieved 13 July 2017.

3.6 Palace and Pavement Where Pilate Judged Jesus.

Jerusalem. Early excavations are by C.N. Johns, starting in 1943. Foundation walls and a sewage system for Herod's palace are found in 2000, below ground underneath a former prison and citadel of the Turks. The team is led by Amit Re'em, of the Israel Antiquities Authority. On the west side of Jerusalem, the palace is not a single building but rather a compound. A palace sometimes is called a *"praetorium"* in gospel translations. Originally a term for the dwelling of a military commander in the field, it means the place where a region's ruler lives. Some traditions place the Roman judgment of Jesus in the Antonia Fortress next to the temple; but this was a barracks for soldiers, not the ruler's residence. It does not fit with the descriptions in the gospel accounts (Mk 15:16; Mt. 27:19, 27; Jn 18:28–33, 19:9, 13). Nor does it fit with the description in Josephus of Roman governors judging on the pavement outside the palace (*War* 2.14.8). Instead, this site on the west side of the upper city fits with both Josephus's description and with John's reference to a *"stone pavement"* or *"gabbatha"* (an Aramaic term). It is an elevated platform, an early attempt at flattening and enlarging a plaza, followed later by the more ambitious project to enlarge the temple mount complex. Herod's Jerusalem palace was built on this stone platform. It was less robustly built than the temple mount foundation and subject to collapse in succeeding decades. The excavation of this site has the unenviable effect of requiring a rerouting of the Via Dolorosa (the commonly regarded route over which Jesus carried his cross beam). Due to tradition and to commercial interests, rerouting is unlikely to happen anytime soon. Be that as it may, the finding supports the detailed account of the trial scene as recounted in the gospel of John. (Jn 18:28, 19:7–16.)

- Ruth Eglash, "Archaeologists find possible site of Jesus' trial in Jerusalem," washingtonpost.com, 4 Jan 2015, *Washington Post, WP Company LLC.*

- Shimon Gibson, "The Trial of Jesus at the Jerusalem Praetorium: New Archaeological Evidence," in Craig A. Evans, ed., *The World of Jesus and the Early Church* (Peabody, MA: Hendrickson Publishers, 2011), 97–118.

- Titus Kennedy, "The Archaeology of a Trial," hopechannel. com, n.d., n.p., retrieved 17 July 2017.

- Jodi Magness, *The Archaeology of the Holy Land* (New York, NY: Cambridge University Press, 2012), 158–59.

- Robin Ngo, "Tour Showcases Remains of Herod's Jerusalem Palace—Possible Site of the Trial of Jesus," biblicalarchaeology.org, Bible History Daily, *Biblical Archaeology Society*, 9 Jan 2016, originally 8 Jan 2015.

- "Antonia Fortress," wikipedia.org, retrieved 17 July 2017.

ҶӀ:

THE DISCIPLES CHANGE FROM FEARFUL
TO BOLD

FINDINGS

4.1 House and Courtyard of High Priest. Jerusalem. Found in 1973, by Israeli Nahman Avigad. Now made part of the Wohl Museum, Jerusalem. It is a large house (6500 sq ft or 600 sq m) or "Herodian mansion" featuring ritual baths, spacious courtyard, easy access and proximity to the temple complex. A geometric investigation confirms there is an angle where Jesus from inside the house could see Peter outside in the courtyard (Lk 22:61). The house was occupied by Annas, the high priest from AD 6–15, who continued to control the priesthood through his five sons and his son-in-law Joseph Caiaphas, the official high priest at the night trial of Jesus. The finding supports the gospel accounts that place Jesus in the house of the high priest after his arrest in the garden. Here he undergoes intense interrogation by the priests. The site also supports the accounts of Peter's denials under public pressure in the courtyard outside the house. (Mk 14:53–72, 15:1; Mt 26:57–75, 27:1–2; Lk 22:54–71, 23:1–2; Jn 18:12–28.)

- Leen Ritmeyer, "The Palace of Annas the High Priest," ritmeyer.com, *Ritmeyer Archaeological Design*, 28 Aug 2012, retrieved 14 July 2017.

- Justin Taylor and contributors, "Is this the High Priestly Palace where Jesus Stood Trial?" blogs.thegospelcoalition. org, *The Gospel Coalition, Inc.*, 28 Aug 2012, retrieved 6 July 2017.

4.2 Ancient Galilee Fishing Boat. Sea of Galilee, Israel. Kept in Yigal Allon Galilee Boat Museum, Kibbutz Ginosar, Israel. Found in 1986 in the mud of the lake, along the northwestern shore, during a rare drought. The boat was discovered by two Israeli fishermen, the brothers Moshe and Yuval Lufan. The vessel is 26.5 ft or 8.3m long and 7.5 ft or 2.3m wide. It is dated to the first century AD due to pottery, a lamp and coins found inside, plus twelve kinds of wood (including cedar, pine, jujube and willow) used in multiple boat repairs. It is possible this vessel crossed nautical paths with boats carrying Jesus. The finding confirms the gospel accounts (and mosaics) of fishing boats that are large enough for sleeping and for transporting 12–15 people. (Mk 4:36–38, 6:30–32, 8:10–13; Jn 6:16–17.)

- Holly Hayes, "Jesus Boat Museum, Tiberias," sacred-destinations.com, *Sacred Destinations*, n.d., retrieved 7 July 2017.

4.3 Galilee Boat Harbors. Sea of Galilee, Israel. Circa 1970–2000. Team led by Mendel Nun. Sixteen ports have been found. The ports include breakwaters, piers, promenades, along with boat anchors, mooring stones, and first-century fishing equipment, such as weights tied to fishing nets. The finding confirms the descriptions of fishing and boat travel in the gospel accounts. (Mk 1:19–20, 4:36, 5:21, 6:54, 8:10; Jn 6:17, 21:3–8.)

- Mendel Nun, "Ports of Galilee," *Biblical Archaeology Review*, 25:04, July/Aug 1999.

4.4 Peter's House in Capernaum. Capernaum, Galilee, Israel. Found in 1968. Italian Franciscan Friars Virgilio Corbo and Stanislao Loffreda discover beneath an octagonal Byzantine church a residence from the first century AD. It is a simple home, clustered around two small courtyards, with the roof having been made of earth and straw. They observe how the main room's function changes within the first century AD, from household cooking to group gatherings with storage jars and oil lamps, and plaster covering the room from floor to ceiling. They conclude a normal house in the harbor town suddenly becomes a place of worship, a telltale sign someone important in the faith had occupied the original residence. The site supports the accounts of Peter, who grew up in Bethsaida, living in Capernaum with his wife and mother-in-law, and working as a commercial fisherman. (Mk 1:16–21, 29–31; Mt 8:14–15; Lk 4:38–39.)

- "The House of Peter: The House of Jesus in Capernaum?" biblicalarchaeology.org, Bible History Daily, *Biblical Archaeology Society*, 3 Mar 2011, retrieved 3 Mar 2017.

- "The Peter's House (sic)," n.a., n.d., capernaum.custodia. org, Sanctuary Capernaum, *Custodia Terrae Sanctae*, retrieved 5 July 2017.

4.5 Bone Box of High Priest. Jerusalem. Found in 1990 by construction workers who randomly open the roof of the tomb by accident with their vehicle. It is identified by Israeli Zvi Greenhut. The elaborately carved limestone box or "ossuary" measures 30 in x 15 in or 75cm x 37cm. Kept in the Israel Museum, Jerusalem. Inscribed on the outside of the box is this name: "Joseph, son of Caiaphas." A few scholars dispute the identification, due to no mention of his high priestly status. Among the bones inside are those of a sixty-year-old male. Joseph, son of Caiaphas, called in the NT simply Caiaphas, presides and leads the questioning of Jesus at the Jewish trial before the assembled teachers and elders. Josephus indicates Caiaphas serves as high priest for eighteen years from AD 18–36 (*Antiquities* 18.26.33–35). The finding supports the NT accounts where Caiaphas is identified by name as a key official or specifically as the current high priest. (Mt 26:3, 57; Lk 3:2; Jn 11:49, 18:13–14, 24, 28; Acts 4:6.)

- Titus Kennedy, "The Archaeology of a Trial," hopechannel. com, *Seventh Day Adventist Church*, 2 Sep 2015, retrieved 14 July 2017.

- Tim Kimberly, "Top Ten Biblical Discoveries in Archaeology—#8 Caiaphas Ossuary," 14 July 2010, credohouse.org, n.p., retrieved 7 July 2017.

- Ronny Reich, "Caiaphas Name Inscribed on Bone Boxes," *Biblical Archaeology Review,* 18:05, Sep/Oct 1992, 38–44.

- "Caiaphas," wikipedia.org, retrieved 14 July 2017.

- "Caiaphas, Joseph," n.a., jewishvirtuallibrary.org, *American-Israeli Cooperative Enterprise*, n.d., retrieved 14 July 2017.

4.6 Italian Regiment Inscription. Caesarea Maritima, Israel. Dated to AD 69. The inscription indicates that a military force stationed in the city was known as the "Second Italian Cohort of Roman Citizen Volunteers." A cohort usually consisted of 480–600 soldiers (six "centuries" of 80–100 soldiers). Most scholars assume it is likely that the cohort was there for many years prior to the inscription. The finding supports the account of Peter being sent for by a centurion based in Caesarea, named Cornelius. (Acts 10:1.)

- John H. Sailhamer, *Biblical Archaeology* (Grand Rapids, MI: Zondervan, 1999), 118.

- Allison A. Trites, *Gospel of Luke* and William J. Larkin, *Acts,* Cornerstone Biblical Commentary, (Carol Stream, IL: Tyndale House Publishers, 2006), 468.

- "Caesarea" and "Acts 10:1," n.a., generationword.com, *Generation Word Church*, n.d., retrieved 15 July 2017.

5:

THE DISCIPLES FACE PERILOUS CULTURAL RISKS

FINDINGS

5.1 The Floor Where Salome Danced. Machaerus, Jordan. The citadel site is found by German Ulrich Seetzen in 1807. The lower city site is found in 1909 by French Dominican father Felix-Marie Abel. Recent excavations have been led by Hungarian Gyozo Voros (with the Hungarian Academy of Arts and the Jordanian Department of Antiquities). The courtyard in the citadel complex offers space for large events with invited guests. The pavement made of stone is the location where Salome dances. The king sits and watches from one side, from the royal throne in a central half-moon niche that is outlined on the floor and can be observed today. The king, Herod Antipas, vows to give the seductive dancer whatever she requests. She asks for the head of John the Baptist on a platter. Already brought in chains to Machaerus, John the Baptist is held and killed, probably in the lower city (*Antiquities* 18.5.2), where his prison is yet to be located in the mounds awaiting excavation. The site confirms the setting for the NT accounts of the royal birthday party gone wild, and tragically wrong. (Mk 6:14–29; Mt 14:6–12.)

- Gyozo Voros, "Machaerus Where Salome Danced and John the Baptist Was Beheaded," and "Anastylosis at Machaerus," in Hershel Shanks, ed., *Herod's Palace*

Fortresses (Wash., DC: Biblical Archaeology Review, 2015), 28–39, 42–43.

5.2 Herodian Theater or Hippodrome. Caesarea Maritima, Israel. The city site is found in 1873 by C. R. Conder and H.H. Kitchener. Herod Agrippa, grandson of Herod the Great, executes James, one of the twelve disciples of Jesus, and imprisons and plans to execute Peter, before the disciple's harrowing escape. Luke narrates Agrippa's comeuppance when he addresses a crowd gathered for games in Caesarea. They worship him as a god, he does not deter them, and he is struck with a fatal condition and dies shortly afterward. This moment might be treated as fictional if not for a parallel account of the event in a secular history, by the Jewish-Roman writer Josephus (*Antiquities* 19.8.2). He adds detail, including that the sun shone in the morning on the dazzling raiment of the king. The moment likely occurs not in the half-moon-shaped drama theater at Caesarea, but rather at the long rectangular amphitheater, or hippodrome, where horse races and combative contests were held. (The Greek word for horse is "hippo".) The morning sun would shine there, but not in the theater; the festivity would be held there, because it involved games not dramas; and Josephus records that fifteen years or so earlier Pilate had conducted his tribunal in the "stadium," a term befitting the hippodrome. This stadium or amphitheater held 20,000 spectators (compared to 4,500 in the drama theater). Remnants of it can be seen today, though recently part of the area reportedly has been used as a banana field. The finding supports Luke's account in Acts of the death of the king who is the first to execute an original disciple. (Acts 12:1–24.)

- Todd Bolen, "Not in the Theater: Challenging Josephus' Location for the Place of Herod Agrippa's Death," bibleinterp.com, *The Bible and Interpretation*, July 2010.

- David Padfield, "The Biblical City of Caesarea Maritima," padfield.com, n.p., 2004.

- "Caesarea," n.a., n.d., jewishvirtuallibrary.org, *American-Israeli Cooperative Enterprise*, retrieved 14 July 2017.

5.3 Tomb of One Philip or Another. Hierapolis, Turkey.
Found in 2011 by Italian Francesco D'Andria. A shrine or "martyrium" has been known for ages marking the death of Philip. About forty yards away, a first-century Roman tomb was discovered below a Byzantine church built around it. Writings on the walls and the structure of the tomb reveal its first-century AD character and its association with Philip. A letter credited to Paul mentions believers in Hierapolis (Col. 4:13). Philip is thought to have died about AD 80 as a martyr, by beheading or crucifixion. No human remains were found; this was not surprising due to traditions holding they were transported to Constantinople and then to Rome. The finding of the tomb supports the gospel accounts of Philip as an approachable, cross-cultural evangelist (Jn 12:20–22) and intensely committed believer (Jn 14:8–9). While the excavators consider it to be the tomb of the *apostle* Philip, one of the twelve original disciples of Jesus, others dispute that conclusion. They take it as more probable that it is the shrine of the *deacon* or *evangelist* Philip, whose adventures are noted at length by Luke (Acts 8:4–8, 26–40, 21:8–9). The Christian church has a long history of conflating the two Philips, so disputes on this order are not surprising. Either way, it is remarkable for an archaeological finding to be able with reasonable certainty to trace its lineage back to a first-generation follower of Jesus.

- Francesco D'Andria, "Conversion, Crucifixion and Celebration," *Biblical Archaeology Review*, 37:04, July/Aug 2011.

- "Philip's Tomb Discovered—But Not Where Expected," n.a., baslibrary.org, *Biblical Archaeology Review*, 38:1, Jan/Feb 2012.

- "Tomb of Apostle Philip Found," n.a. (staff), Bible History Daily, *Biblical Archaeology Society*, 6 Jan 2017, originally published Jan 2012.

- "Tomb of St. Philip the Apostle Discovered in Turkey," n.a., foxnews.com, Fox News Tech, *Fox News Digital*, 27 July 2011, retrieved 15 July 2017.

ⓑ:

A FIERCE ENFORCER SWITCHES SIDES

FINDINGS

(Note: Corinth-related findings from Paul's journeys are discussed in Chapter 7.)

6.1 Temple Warning Inscriptions. Jerusalem. These plaques function as "Do Not Enter" or "Off Limits" warning signs. The first one is found in 1871 by French archaeologist Charles Simon Clermont-Ganneau. It was embedded in a wall of a Muslim school in the Old City of Jerusalem, about 164 ft or 50m from the temple mount. Kept in Istanbul Archaeology Museum, Instanbul, Turkey. In size, it is 22 in x 33 in or 56cm x 84cm, with letters 1.5 in or 4cm high. This sign was written in red ink against the white background of the limestone. It warns that any trespasser will invite death should he go beyond the three-foot or one-meter high boundary wall marking the point from which non-Jews could go no further toward the temple (Acts 21:27–29). Written in seven lines in Greek, one translation reads: _No foreigner is to go beyond the balustrade and the plaza of the temple zone. Whoever is caught doing so will have himself to blame for his death which will follow._ (See "Temple Warning Inscription," n.a., bible-history.com, _Bible History Online_, n.d.) A second sign, only partially in tact, was found in 1935, during an excavation in a tomb outside the Lion's Gate. Kept in the Israel Museum, Jerusalem. It confirms the mention of signs in Josephus (_War_ 5.5.2, 6.2.4, _Antiquities_ 15.11.3) and supports the account in Acts of the false accusations against Paul for supposedly trespassing this boundary with a non-Jew traveling companion, Trophimus from Ephesus. (Acts 21:27–30.)

- Ilan Ben Zion, "Ancient Temple Mount 'Warning' Stone is 'Closest thing we have to the Temple'," timesofisrael.com, *The Times of Israel*, 22 Sep 2015, retrieved 8 July 2017.

- Rick Gladstone, "Historical Certainty Proves Elusive at Jerusalem's Holiest Place," 8 Oct 2015, mobile.nytimes. com, *The New York Times*, retrieved 8 July, 2017.

- "Soreg, Middle wall of Partition, Herod's Temple, Jerusalem, Israel," n.a., biblicalgeographic.com, *Biblical Geographic*, 2011, retrieved 31 Oct 2017.

6.2 The Damascus Street Called "Straight." Damascus, Syria. This heralded ancient street in Damascus continues to be a main thoroughfare to this day and goes by the same name. The Romans arrive in the first century BC. They use the term *"Via Recta"* for the street and add a theater at one end. This setting supports the account by Luke in Acts that names this street as the location where Paul was taken after his eyes were blinded on the road to Damascus. Here at the house of a disciple named Judas, Paul would meet a resident Jesus follower named Ananias, who would restore his sight and arrange for Paul to be baptized. After meeting other disciples, Paul shortly began preaching in the synagogue and proving Jesus was the Messiah, until death threats drove him from the city. (Acts 9:10–25.)

- Rania Abouzeid, "Syria's War, And Its Past, On a Street Called Straight," 24 Dec 2013, newyorker.com, *The New Yorker*, retrieved 9 July 2017.

- Ross Burns, *Origins of the Colonnaded Streets in the Cities of the Roman East* (Oxford, UK: Oxford University Press, 2017), 162.

- John H. Sailhamer, *Biblical Archaeology* (Grand Rapids, MI: Zondervan, 1998), 118.

6.3 Inscriptions of Cyprus Official Who Believes. Cyprus. The first of three inscriptions is found at Soli, Cyprus in 1877 by Italian-American Colonel Luigi Palma di Cesnola, while serving as American consul in Cyprus. It includes only the "Paulus" part of the official's name, in Greek. A second plaque found in Kythraia, Cyprus, also by di Cesnola, gives the full name, "Quintus Sergius Paulus," dated to the time of the emperor Claudius. Kept in the Metropolitan Museum of Art, New York, NY. A third inscription found in 1887 in Rome records that Sergius Paulus was one of the managers of the riverbanks and the channel of the Tiber River, a position he could have held before or after serving as proconsul in Cyprus. It is written in Latin. These findings support the account in Acts of the first Roman ruler converted to Christian faith by Paul during his first missionary journey, on Cyprus. (Acts 13:6–12.)

- Joseph N. Holden and Norman Geisler, *The Popular Handbook of Archaeology and the Bible* (Eugene, OR: Harvest House Publishers, 2013), 352–53.

- "Inscriptions Confirming Sergius Paulus," n.a., n.d., literature-middle-ages.com, retrieved 8 July 2017.

- "Luigi Palma di Cesnola," wikipedia.org, retrieved 16 July 2017.

- "Sergius Paulus," n.a., biblehistory.net, n.p., 2013, retrieved 30 July 2017.

6.4 Egnatian Way. Albania, North Macedonia, Greece, Turkey. This was Rome's major road to link its capital city to its colonies in the east. The road began on the east side of the Adriatic Sea, almost opposite of the terminus of the Appian Way on the other side of the sea at Brindisi, so that ships could take the shortest route. The road crossed over the Jablanica mountain ridge and lake country to the coastline of Greece, first at Thessalonica and then north through Greece on to Byzantium, later renamed Constantinople, and now known as Istanbul. The road was built in the second century BC, at the orders of Gnaeus Egnatius, proconsul of Macedonia. The total distance spanned was 696 miles or 1,020 km. The finding of the route supports Paul's reported itinerary through Neopolis, Philippi, Amphipolis, Apollonia and Thessalonica, traveling east to west (Acts 16:11–12, 17:1).

- "Via Egnatia," wikipedia.org, retrieved 8 July 2017.

6.5 Temple of Artemis. Ephesus, Turkey. The site is found in 1863 by British railway engineer and architect John Turtle Wood. The early site is dated from the sixth century BC. The first temple structure is built by King Croesus of Lydia, then expanded by the Greeks in the second century BC. Later excavations determine that the temple had a platform 425 ft long x 220 ft wide, or 130m x 67m. It had 127 Ionic columns, each one 60 ft tall x 7 ft in diameter, or 18m x 2m. It was four times the size of the Parthenon in Athens, befitting a city that competed with Antioch to be the third largest in the Roman world after Rome and Alexandria. This finding confirms the rationale for the reported rioting against Paul when his preaching threatens the tourist-trapping shrine. (Acts 19:23–41.)

- James R. Edwards, "Archaeology Gives New Reality to Paul's Ephesian Riot," *Biblical Archaeology Review*, 42:04, July/Aug 2016, 24–32, 62.

- "Ephesus," n.a., n.d., ephesus.us, *Ephesus Ancient City*, Selcuk, Turkey, retrieved 18 July 2017.

6.6 Statues of Artemis. Ephesus, Turkey. Found in 1956 by Viennese Franz Miltner. The two most famous statues are known as the "Great Artemis" and the "Beautiful Artemis." Kept in the Ephesus Archaeological Museum, Selcuk, Turkey. These versions are dated to the second century AD, 50 to 100 years after Paul's time in Ephesus. Artemis (the Greek name, with Diana the Roman name) is the goddess of the hunt, wild animals, forests and wilderness, and came to be associated with childbirth and motherhood. The oval pendants that are clustered to form a necklace or sash around each of these statues of Artemis were once thought to be breasts, or ostrich eggs, or fruit; now they are considered more likely to be bull or even more probably stag testicles, trophies of her silver bow and arrow, indicating the divine feminine dominance of virility. These findings support the account by Luke in Acts for the broad popularity throughout the region claimed by proponents of the Artemis religion. (Acts 19:27–28.)

- James R. Edwards, "Archaeology Gives New Reality to Paul's Ephesian Riot," *Biblical Archaeology Review*, 42:04, July/Aug 2016, 24–32, 62.

6.7 *Commercial Shops and Agora.* Ephesus, Turkey. Diagonally across the main street from the theater, in a large square 360 ft x 360 ft, or 110m x 110m, a series of shop units filled three sides, in an early mall of sorts. The site confirms the account in Acts that there were many shop-owners in Ephesus who felt threatened by Paul's preaching against the religion of Artemis. Their trade in crafting mini-shrines and idols of silver would be severely hurt if people were to believe gods made of hands were no gods at all. (Acts 19:23–27.)

- James S. Jeffers, *The Greco-Roman World of the New Testament Era* (Downers Grove, IL: InterVarsity Press, 1999), 268.

- "Ephesus, Commercial Agora," n.a., livius.org, n.p., n.d.

6.8 *Riotous Theater.* Ephesus, Turkey. Dated from the third century BC, it was built by the Greeks during the reign of Lysimachus, and later expanded by the Romans. The large, semi-circular, limestone, open-air theater seated 25,000 people for dramas, religious services, public events, and bloody battle contests. The expanded edifice is dated from AD 40. The site supports the account of shop-owners and others gathering at the nearby theater to protest before government officials about the radical Paul, who was speaking against their goddess Artemis and jeopardizing their trade in trinkets honoring her. (Acts 19:8-10, 23-41.)

- James R. Edwards, "Archaeology Gives New Reality to Paul's Ephesian Riot," *Biblical Archaeology Review*, 42:04, July/Aug 2016, 24–32, 62.

- Amanda Hefferman, "The Theatre at Ephesus (near Selcuk, Turkey)," 2003, whitman.edu, *The Ancient Theatre Archive, Whitman College*, ed. 15 Feb 2009, retrieved 8 July 2017.

6.9 _Evidence for the Antonia Fortress._ Jerusalem. Northwest of and adjacent to the temple complex. No ruins have been unearthed, only cuts indicating foundation lines have been detected. The descriptions of the site come mainly from Josephus (*War* 1.21.1, 5.5.8 and *Antiquities* 15.8.5, 15.11.4, 18.4.3). The fortress was built before 31 BC, by Herod the Great, in honor of his patron at the time, Marc Antony, who later lost the competition to become Roman emperor to Octavian, later known as Augustus. The building served as a barracks for a cohort of Roman soldiers in Jerusalem (a cohort usually featured 480–600 soldiers). The fortress location served to repel enemy attacks that usually came from the north, and to control the often volatile temple mount crowds. The stone "fort" had four sides, sprouting towers on each corner, with a taller tower on the southeast corner overlooking the temple plaza. In the NT, a mob falsely accuses Paul of defiling the temple by bringing into the inner courts his uncircumcised Greek companion Trophimus. Roman soldiers lift Paul out of the crowd and start to carry him into the fortress for his own safety (Acts

21:35). Paul asks their commander if he can address the crowd from the steps rising to the fortress entrance. The site layout and descriptions support the account of the near-riot and rescue of Paul. (Acts 21:27–40, 22:1–30, 23:10.)

- Ehud Netzer, "A New Reconstruction of Paul's Prison," *Biblical Archaeology Review,* 35:1, Jan/Feb 2009, 44–51, 71. Available at baslibrary.org, *Biblical Archaeology Society,* retrieved 17 July 2017.

- "Antonia Fortress," wikipedia.org, retrieved 17 July 2017.

6.10 Palace Where Paul Appeals to Caesar. Caesarea Maritima, Israel. Site of Herod's seaside palace. The Roman governor Felix orders that Paul *"be kept under guard in Herod's palace"* (Acts 23:35). It is not a bad spot for a staycation. Herod built his palace on a promontory arcing into the ocean, south of the harbor. It is the best place to catch cooling breezes. Pool is included. Occupants see the ships sailing in from the sea. Excavations reveal rooms where Paul may have been held in confinement, one of which had an ocean and harbor view to the north. There are stone floors in the large audience hall of the palace, which can be seen today; they are likely the scene for Paul's hearing before the authorities. Earlier, Paul had been a semi-frequent pass-through tourist in Caesarea. He had escaped an earlier murder squad in Jerusalem when friends had sent him off by ship to Tarsus (Acts 9:30). After his second journey, he lands at Caesarea, before heading inland to Jerusalem (Acts 18:22). In this last visit, he is brought to the Roman coastal city under armed guard for his own safety when Jerusalem priests demand his trial. He is held in custody for two years, until he appeals to Caesar. After a hearing, he is sent to Rome about AD 59. (Acts 25:11–14, 25.)

- David Padfield, "The Biblical City of Caesarea Maritima," padfield.com, n.d., retrieved 7 July 2017.

- Joseph Patrick, *Studies in the Archaeology and History of Caesarea Maritima*, Caput Judaeae, Metropolis Palaestinae, (Leiden, The Netherlands: Kininklijke Brill, 2011).

- "Caesarea Maritima–Israel," 22 Aug 2015, n.a., cannundrum.blogspot.com, *Cannundrums*, retrieved 16 July 2017.

- John J. Rousseau and Rami Arav, *Jesus and His World: An Archaeological and Cultural Dictionary* (Minneapolis, MN: Fortress Press, 1995).

6.11 The Renowned Roman Road, the Appian Way. Italy. The major Roman road in Italy. First built in 312 BC by Appius Claudius Caecus. The distance it eventually traversed was 350 miles or 563 km from the Roman Forum to the southeastern port of Brundisium (modern Brindisi) on the western shore of the Adriatic Sea. From there ships would embark for Greece or for the eastern Mediterranean. The road was about 20 ft or 6m wide with a slight convex shape on the surface to facilitate drainage into ditches on either side. The road's foundation consisted of heavy stone blocks with lime mortar serving as cement between the blocks. On top of these blocks, lava stones were laid in interlocking patterns to provide a durable road surface. The finding supports the account in Acts of Paul's landing by ship at Puetoli (modern Pozzuoli near Naples), the key Roman port for importing grain from Egypt. He then travels 170 miles or 274 km along the Appian Way to Rome. Paul is met by friends about 43 miles or 69 km from Rome at the Forum of Appias, by more friends about 12 miles or 20 km closer to Rome, and finally by even more friends at the Three Taverns (or "Inns" or "Shops" in some translations). (Acts 28:13–16.)

- "Appian Way," britannica.com, *Encyclopedia Britannica*, n.d., retrieved 8 July 2017.

- "Appian Way" and "Pozzuoli," wikipedia.org, retrieved 8 July 2017.

7:

PROCLAMATION OF THE RESURRECTION
IS CLEARLY EARLY

FINDINGS

7.1 Erastus Inscription. Corinth, Greece. Found in 1929 by land excavators, the inscription is carved into a limestone paving stone, with big letters, 7 in or 18cm high, originally inlaid with metal that was probably bronze. Dated to the first century AD. Kept in place in pavement at Corinth, northeast of the theater. It signifies that Erastus, in return for his position (in Latin, the office of "aedilis") paved this section of the road at his own expense. When Paul writes the letter to the Romans, he resides in Corinth or in the nearby port town of Cenchrae. Among his companions who send along their greetings is Erastus, whom Paul identifies as Corinth's *"director of public works,"* sometimes translated as "city treasurer." Regardless of the exact title, the inscription supports the name of this friend of Paul and Paul's assertion that he serves in a high-ranking municipal position. Skeptics question whether the persons are one and the same, but it is more probable that they are the same person, given the official's high standing (Acts 19:22; Rom. 16:23; 1 Tim. 4:20).

- Victor Paul Furnish, "Corinth in Paul's Time—What Can Archaeology Tell Us?" *Biblical Archaeology Review*, 14:03, May/June 1988, 15-27.

- "Corinth in History and Archaeology," n.a., ap.lanexdev. com, apologeticspress.org, *Apologetics Press*, 2003, retrieved 20 July 2017.

- Jefferson White, "Erastus: Treasurer of Corinth," pauls-journeys.com, from the book, Jefferson White, *Evidence and Paul's Journeys* (n.a.: Parsagard Press, 2001).

- F.F. Bruce, *The Epistle of Paul to the Romans* (Grand Rapids, MI: Wm. B. Eerdmans, 1982), 280.

- Joseph N. Holden and Norman Geisler, *The Popular Handbook of Archaeology and the Bible* (Eugene, OR: Harvest House Publishers, 2013), 358–59.

7.2 Gallio or Delphi Inscription. Delphi, Achaia, Greece. The first limestone fragments are found in 1885 in Delphi, Greece by Adolf Deissman. The finding is popularized in 1905 by Emile Bourget, who documented the first four fragments. Nine fragments found over several decades formed a puzzle that finally showed all pieces were from the same original inscription. Kept in Ecole Francais d'archeologie, Athens, Greece. The inscription recounts a letter from the emperor Claudius commending Gallio as proconsul of Achaia. Using the Roman calendar system, it is dated to AD 52 (see chapter 7 in the main book). The finding confirms the presence of the prominent Roman official Gallio in Corinth in AD 52. With a cross-reference to Luke's account, this finding confirms that Paul is in Corinth and causing synagogue riots in that time frame. Verified by both literary and archaeological evidence, this date anchors Paul's chronology. (Acts 18:12–17.)

- K.C. Hanson, "The Gallio Inscription," kchanson.com, K.C. Hanson's Collection of Greek Documents, retrieved 20 Aug 2017.

- Joseph N. Holden and Norman Geisler, *The Popular Handbook of Archaeology and the Bible* (Eugene, OR: Harvest House Publishers, 2013), 357.

- Jerome Murphy-O'Connor, *St. Paul's Corinth: Texts and Archaeology*, Good News Studies, Vol. 6, (Wilmington, DE: Michael Glazier, 1987), 141–52, plus Appendix, 173–76.

7.3 Judgment Platform or Bema. Corinth, Greece. Found in 1935 by a Greek government project and identified in 1937 by Swedish-American archaeologist Oscar Broneer. The platform is made of marble stones. It is called a "bema" in Greek and a "rostra" or "rostrum" in Latin. It partially stands to this day in a prominent place in the Roman forum of Corinth, with a high hill rising behind it, known as the Acrocorinth. The inscription on the bema dates its origin to the reign of Augustus or Claudius, within the time span AD 25–50, before Paul first comes to Corinth. It is likely that this is the exact spot where Gallio heard Paul's accusers, and dismissed the case. It supports the account in Acts that the area could contain an agitated crowd. An alternative site for the hearing suggested by some scholars is the Julian basilica one block away, the remains of which also have been unearthed. (Acts 18:12-17.)

- John McRay, *Archaeology & the New Testament* (Grand Rapids, MI: Baker Academic, Baker Publishing Group, 1991), 335.

- Seth M. Rodriquez, "Picture of the Week: The Bema at Corinth," blog.bibleplaces.com, *Bible Places*, 1 Aug 2013, retrieved 20 July 2017.

- "Corinth in History and Archaeology," n.a., ap.lanexdev. com, apologeticspress.org, *Apologetics Press*, 2003, retrieved 20 July 2017.

8:

JERUSALEM REMAINS THE EPICENTER OF THE MESSAGE

FINDINGS

8.1 Trumpeting Inscription. Jerusalem. Found in 1968 by Israeli Benjamin Mazar near the south wall of the temple mount. The finding appears on a block of basalt stone of this size: 33 in x 12 in x 10 in or 84cm x 31cm x 26cm. Kept in Israel Museum, Jerusalem. The inscription captures two complete Hebrew words, reading in translation "to the place" and "of trumpeting." It is believed to be a capstone for a tower wall. The inscription was a directional sign for priests to find the exact spot where they were to blow the trumpet to signal the beginning of the Sabbath day at sunset, and its end at twilight the next day. When in Jerusalem, Jesus and his disciples would hear the trumpet sounding from this place. The custom is mentioned by Josephus (*War* 4.9.12).

- *Rose Book of Bible Charts, Maps & Timelines*, n.a., (Torrance, CA: Rose Publishing, 2005). Also available at rose-publishing.com.

- "Trumpeting Place Inscription," wikipedia.org, retrieved 30 July 2017.

8.2 Western Wall. Jerusalem. Southwestern wall. Known in Hebrew as "Kotel ha-Ma'aravi." It is made of limestone. The wall's length is 1600 ft or 488m, while the wall's height varies with the terrain of the bedrock. Currently the wall's highest point is 131 ft or 40m above *bedrock*. In the area of the prayer plaza, the wall is 62 ft or 19m above ground—though if the wall is measured from its foundation below ground it would be considered 104 ft or 32m high. Originally, the wall may have towered over bedrock reaching as high as 196 ft or 60m. The wall is the only remaining structure from the "second temple," the temple built by Zerubbabel (Ezra 4:3, Zech. 4:9), then renovated into greater splendor by Herod the Great, as opposed to the famous "first temple" which was built by Solomon. This western wall is not a wall of the temple or any building that stood on the temple complex. It is a set of large stones functioning as a retaining wall, which Herod built to enlarge greatly the esplanade or plaza to create a wide flat space on the temple mount. After 1967, the wall became a prayer and pilgrimage site for reverent Jewish believers. The finding of these large retaining walls supports the gospel accounts of expansive areas on the temple mount where crowds could gather to hear Jesus teach, and later to see the disciples preach and get themselves arrested (Mk 11:27, 12:35, 41; Jn 7:14, 28, 18:20; Acts 2:46, 4:1–4). The stones stacked on top of one another do not negate Jesus's prediction that no stone would remain left upon another. That historically accurate prediction applied to *buildings* on the site, not to the *retaining walls* (Mk 13:1–2; Mt 24:1–2; Lk 21:5–6).

- "The Western Wall: History and Overview", n.a., jewishvirtuallibrary.org, *American-Israeli Cooperative Enterprise*, n.d., retrieved 14 July 2017.

- "What is the Western Wall?" n.a., english.thekotel.org, *The Western Wall Heritage Foundation*, n.d., retrieved 15 July 2017.

8.3 Arch of Titus South Panel Relief. Rome, Italy. The famous arch has stood on the Palatine Hill for nearly two millennia.

Dated to AD 82. The full arch stands 50 ft or 15.4m in height, 44 ft or 13.5m in length and 15.5 ft or 4.75m in width. The south panel relief on stone depicts the Roman general Titus Vespasian destroying Jerusalem in AD 70. It shows telltale symbols of victory over the Jews. The spoils of war include a menorah, trumpets, fire pans used for catching ashes from the temple altar, and the table of showbread. The arch was constructed to honor the victories of Titus by his younger brother, Emperor Domitian. The design serves as a template for other arches built to memorialize historical events, among them the Arc de Triomphe in Paris, France. The panel relief confirms the success of the Roman siege, supporting the heart-rending predictions Jesus made about the future destruction of Jerusalem. (Lk 19:41–44, 21:5–6, 21–24; Mk 13:1–2.)

- "Arch of Titus" and "List of artifacts significant to biblical archaeology," wikipedia.org, retrieved 30 July 2017.

8.4 Temple Sundial. Jerusalem. Found in 1972 by Israeli Benjamin Mazar. This limestone sundial is left behind by the Romans in the rubble, after the destruction of the temple in AD 70. Kept in Hecht Museum, Haifa, Israel. The sundial face is calibrated to tell time and seasons from the vantage point of Jerusalem. Engraved on the reverse side is a seven-branched menorah. The sundial was used by priests to perform rituals at scheduled times. The finding supports the destruction of the temple area by the Romans, as predicted by Jesus (Lk 19:41–44).

- Benjamin Mazar and Gaalyahu Cornfeld, *The Mountain of the Lord* (Garden City, New York: Doubleday, 1975).

8.5 Inscription on the Reign of David. Tel Dan, Israel. Found in 1993–94 in northern Israel near the base of Mount Hermon. It is discovered by the surveyor and architect Gila Cook, with her team led by Israeli Avraham Biran. Dated to the ninth century BC. Kept in the Israel Museum, Jerusalem. It is written in early

Aramaic with the Phoenician alphabet, on black basalt stone in three fragments. On the stone "stele," an Aramaean king recounts how he defeats in battle two southern neighbors, which he identifies as "the king of Israel" and the "king of the House of David." The names of the kings are not mentioned. Scholars figure it is probably Hazael of Damascus celebrating the defeat of Joram of Israel and Ahaziah of Judah (2 Kings 8:28–29, 10:32, 13:3, 22). This is the first archaeological evidence discovered that affirms the existence of King David, a major figure in the OT writings. It shows a century after David's death he continues to be recognized as a significant enemy of the Arameans. The finding definitively confirms that King David was an actual historical figure, not a fictional creation of the OT writers and/or editors. (2 Sam. 8:6; 1 Chron. 18:6; Acts 2:22–36, 13:34–37.)

- "'David' Found at Dan," n.a., *Biblical Archaeology Review*, 20:02, Mar/April 1994. Available at cojs.org, *Center for Online Judaic Studies*.

- "The Tel Dan Inscription: The First Historical Evidence of King David from the Bible," bibilicalarchaeology.org, Bible History Daily, *Biblical Archaeology Society*, 8 Nov 2016, retrieved 7 July 2017.

- "Avraham Biran," conservapedia.com, retrieved 15 July 2017.

- Avraham Biran and Joseph Naveh, "An aramaic stele fragment from Tel Dan," *Israel Exploration Journal*, Vol. 43, Nos. 2–3, 1993. Available at berlinarchaeology.files. wordpress.com.

- "Tel Dan Stele," wikipedia.org, retrieved 30 July 2017.

- Gila Cook, "How I Discovered the 'House of David' Inscription," ngsba.org, The Nelson Glueck School of

Biblical Archaeology, *Hebrew Union College-Jewish Institute of Religion*, n.d., retrieved 15 July 2017.

- "Tel Dan Stele.", newworldencyclopedia.org, *New World Encyclopedia*, 24 Nov 2008, 21:14 UTC, retrieved 31 July 2017.

8.6 Rock of Abraham. Jerusalem. Kept in the Islamic shrine known as the Dome of the Rock. This shrine was initiated by the Umayyad Islamic emperor, Abd al-Malik ibn Marwan (AD 646–705), and completed in AD 692. The rock is 60 ft x 40 ft or 18m x 12m and rises 6 ft or 2m from the floor of the surrounding building. The building is not a mosque but a shrine. A mosque lies nearby, called the Al-Aqsa Mosque (meaning "the farthest mosque"), and the Muslim area is known as Al-Haram ash-Sharif or "the noble sanctuary." The rock is positioned at the highest point on the hill, known as Mount Moriah. It is believed to be the location where Abraham prepared to sacrifice his son Isaac (Gen. 22:1–14). Also, it is believed by some to be the location for the threshing floor of Araunah, the Jebusite, who allowed David to buy the land and build an altar to the Lord (2 Sam. 24:18). In addition, the rock may have been the floor for the sacred room known as the Holy of Holies in the first temple of Solomon and the second temple in its refurbished state under Herod the Great.

- "Question: What is the Dome of the Rock?" n.a. gotquestions.org, *Got Questions Ministries*, n.d., retrieved 15 July 2017.

- "Dome of the Rock," brittanica.com, *Encyclopedia Britannica*, n.d., retrieved 15 July 2017.

॥ ९ ॥

GOSPEL ACCOUNTS CORRELATE WITH MESSIANIC PROPHECIES

FINDINGS

9.1 Isaiah Scroll from the Cave Near the Dead Sea.
Qumran, West Bank. One of the collection known as "the Dead Sea Scrolls"(abbreviated "DSS" or "dss"). First located in 1946 in Qumran, Jordan, the site now is part of the West Bank, and is overseen by Israel. It is one mile or 1.6 km inland from the northwest shore of the Dead Sea. These are the Isaiah scroll dimensions: 24 ft or 734cm long by 11 in or 28cm wide, with 54 columns of text on the parchment. It was found in a cave in an earthen jar by teenage Arab Bedouin shepherds Muhammed edh-Dhib, Jum'a Muhammed, and Khalil Musa. They were searching for a lost sheep.

This nearly complete copy of the book of Isaiah was found in the initial cave, along with six other manuscripts. Eventually (from 1946–56), parts of every OT book were found except for Esther, among the more than 1,000 manuscripts in twelve caves. Other documents included sectarian writings for the community, considered by most scholars to be comprised of a people known as the Essenes. The scrolls mainly were written in Hebrew, with some documents in Aramaic and Greek. They are dated in the range from 300 BC to AD 100 and kept in the Shrine of the Book, the Israel Museum, Jerusalem. The initial scrolls were passed on by the shepherds to antiquities dealers, then to the Syrian orthodox bishop; finally they were bought by Israeli archaeologist Yigael Yadin in 1954. The astonishing finding radically pushed back the date by more than 1,000 years for the earliest Hebrew-language manuscripts of the OT books, from the Masoretic text circa tenth century AD to the Dead Sea Scrolls circa second century BC. Surprisingly, few differences emerged between the texts, beyond minor grammatical changes. The rarity of discrepancies verified the sustained quality of meticulous copying in Israelite culture. The finding confirms that the prophecies of Isaiah were written 500–700 years before Jesus, and could not have been retrojected by the gospel writers or later Christians.

- "The Great Isaiah Scroll," dss.collections.imj.org.il, *The Digital Dead Sea Scrolls*, n.d., retrieved 7 July 2017.

- "Isaiah Scroll," wikipedia.org, retrieved 7 July 2017.

9.2 Modest House in Nazareth. Nazareth, Israel. Found in 2009 by a team led by Israeli archaeologist Yardenna Alexandre. Her team excavated a house with two rooms and a courtyard, with a water cistern hewn from rock. The size of the house was at least 900 sq ft or 85 sq m. No adorning mosaics or frescoes were found, which meant that the house was for people of modest means. In surrounding areas, the evidence shows work activity in vineyards, terraced farming, stone masonry, grape and olive presses, reflecting scenes captured vividly in the teachings of Jesus. The finding confirms that Nazareth was populated during the time of Jesus, contradicting prior claims that the village was deserted during the early part of the first century AD. (Mk 1:9; Mt 21:11; Lk 2:4, 39, 4:16; Jn 1:45–46, 18:5–8, 19:19; Acts 2:22, 3:6, 4:10, 10:38, 22:8, 26:9.)

- Patrick J. Kiger, "Archaeological Finds from the Jesus Era," nationalgeographic.com, *National Geographic Channel*, 27 Feb 2015, retrieved 26 July 2017.

- "A Residential Building from the Time of Jesus," n.a., archaeology.org.il, *The Friends of the Israel Antiquities Authority*, n.d., retrieved 22 Oct 2017.

JESUS SAID TO HER, "I AM THE RESURRECTION AND THE LIFE. THE ONE WHO BELIEVES IN ME WILL LIVE, EVEN THOUGH THEY DIE; AND WHOEVER LIVES BY BELIEVING IN ME WILL NEVER DIE. DO YOU BELIEVE THIS?"

— *Jesus of Nazareth, circa AD 30-31 a few days before his crucifixion, to his friend and host Martha of Bethany, as quoted in John 11:25–26 (NIV)*

Printed in the United States
By Bookmasters